In My EYE

In My Eye

Pentecost Explained

STEPHEN MANLEY

Cross Style Press

IN MY EYE: PENTECOST EXPLAINED
© 2018 by Stephen Manley

First Published 2009
Revised Edition 2018

Published by Cross Style Press
Lebanon, Tennessee
CrossStyle.org

Edited by Delphine Manley

ISBN-10: 0-9987265-6-7
ISBN-13: 978-0-9987265-6-4

Printed in the United States of America.

CrossStyle.org

CONTENTS

1

LISTEN TO ME

ACTS 2:14

The Pentecost event (Acts 2:1-4) shakes the known and the unknown world. Things will never be the same again. Data and organized facts make little difference. But truth changes things forever! Once truth is realized, there is no turning back. Man lost what God intended for him in creation, and now God is restoring His original plan. Man is again filled with the Spirit of God. We have a copy of the very first message designed to explain the new level. Can you imagine the tone of such a sermon? Think of the expression on Peter's face as he preached this message to those gathered. Hear the boldness in his delivery.

Peter is preaching to the great crowd gathered at the Pentecost event. The atmosphere is filled with the strength of the Spirit. Make no mistake, everyone present is aware of something great. It is so unmistakable that all are jarred at the outset of the message. Luke goes overboard in his language to make us aware that this is not a normal preaching engagement. A brand new thing is happening. Man is being moved to a different level. It is the new level of Pentecost.

Luke uses three verses to introduce Peter's sermon (Acts 2:14-16). In the first of these verses (verse 14) he gives us the TONE of the address. In the second verse (verse 15) he reveals the correction or TRUTH as delivered by Peter. The third verse (verse 16) is an introduction to the TEXT from Joel which forms the base of Peter's message.

The actual delivery of the sermon is an important element in the communication of the message. Preaching the Gospel and lecturing on other subjects are distinctly different. Lectures have to do with the sharing of information and data, and they focus on the academic process. But the Gospel message is not on that level. Preaching has to do with the flow of the Spirit of Christ. However, it is the flow of the Spirit through the preacher which creates the force of the message. In a real sense the preacher is to become the message! It must be a fire in his very bones and spill from his heart.

Luke highlights this element repeatedly in these verses. To state the tone of the message, he writes, *But Peter, standing up with the eleven, raised his voice and said to them, "Men of Judea and all who dwell in Jerusalem, let this be known to you, and heed my words,"* (Acts 2:14). "I want to share with you" is a phrase which does not even begin to describe this preaching event. "Let us pause to briefly consider the Word," is not a proper description of this message. Peter stands before this crowd with a great proclamation. It can never be described as a devotional.

Let's begin with this, *But Peter, standing up with the eleven.* The Greek word translated *standing* is used in a variety of ways, one hundred and fifty-four times in the New Testament. It refers to a position of the body

(Matthew 6:5), the ceasing or stopping of something that is moving (Matthew 2:9), and to stand firm or resist (Matthew 12:25). In our passage, this verb is in the form of a participle. It acts as an adverb giving content to the two main verbs which follow. What is really startling is that it is in the passive voice. This means that the subject is not responsible for the action but is receiving the action of the verb. At first view this seems a bit strange. One would certainly think that Peter is responsible for standing up before the crowd, but something is acting upon Peter. Luke tells us that this happening is not the average sharing of information. Peter is not standing as he has done so many other times to enter into another argument. He is not defending or protecting his position. One cannot look at this scene and say, "There Peter goes again. No one needs to pay attention to him." In light of the context we know that the Holy Spirit has placed Peter on his feet. This pronouncement is on a very high level.

The same thing takes place as Peter is placed before the council (Acts 4:7). After spending the night in jail, Peter is brought before the leadership of Israel. They ask for an explanation of the miracle which took place yesterday (Acts 3:7). Peter is filled with the Holy Spirit (Acts 4:8) and begins to preach to them. Again Luke tells us this happening is very significant. This is not just the ranting and raving of a man who is under pressure. Peter is not spilling out his carnal self-centeredness. This message is from another source!

There are two main verbs presented to us in our verse. The first one is **raised**. The meaning of this word is far beyond the idea of shouting. It literally means "to lift up." It is used to describe the ascension of Jesus Christ

9

to the right hand of the Father (Acts 1:9). It contains the action of a sail being hoisted up (Acts 27:40). The truth which is to be proclaimed must be lifted up above all other ideas and concepts. Above all earthly explanations (Acts 2:13) or personal expression, the truth of this new level must be seen and heard. What is happening is not on the level of just another gathering. God takes charge of Peter and his voice becomes the instrument which lifts up the message above all others.

We now come to the third statement. It is the second verb in our text, and it is so strong that it elevates this scene above all others. *But Peter, standing up with the eleven, raised His voice and said to them,* (Acts 2:14). The Greek word translated *said* is only used three times in the New Testament. All three times are found in the Book of Acts (2:4; 2:14; 29:25). This is the same word Luke used to describe the speaking of the Holy Spirit through the disciples in languages they did not know (Acts 2:4). It was a Divine utterance! Paul was confronted by Festus as he was defending his *heavenly vision* before King Agrippa (Acts 26:19). Festus accused him of being out of his mind (crazy). Paul replied, *"I am not mad, most noble Festus, but speak the words of truth and reason,"* (Acts 26:25). This Greek word means "to speak out loudly and clearly, or with emphasis." It is used in connection with philosophers and prophets. In the Old Testament it is used for the speech of the wise man, the fortune-teller.

It is easy to see what Luke's intentions are! He sets the tone and atmosphere for this first public explanation of the new level to which God has brought Christianity! He does it by the use of three words which form the context of the delivery of this message. The first is *standing,* the second is *raised,* and the third is *said.* Do you realize this combination is not used any other place in the New Testament to emphasize any other message? The disciples are experiencing a new level and it is like nothing anyone has ever witnessed. What is happening to and in the disciples cannot be contained in the average, normal, casual conversation. The indwelt Christ demands a completely new style of communication.

In Peter's next statement to the crowd we see that he recognizes what is taking place and the high importance or status of his message. He said, *"Men of Judea and all who dwell in Jerusalem, let this be known to you, and heed my words,"* (Acts 2:14). There are two parallel statements: *let this be known to you* and *heed my words.* These two verbal expressions are really only emphatic supplements, one of the other. They do not actually introduce any new information.

In the first phrase, the verb is *be.* It is an imperative which sets the tone for the entire statement. It expresses the intensity which is found within Peter as he is an instrument for the explanation, the truth. It is imperative they understand what he is going to explain. This is not optional; it is absolutely necessary. What Peter has experienced and is going to invite others to participate in cannot be casually presented. This is not on the level of a salesman who is trying to make a living. This is the desperation of a heart that has seen truth. How can the message come forth without being a command?

The second phrase immediately follows: *heed my words.* The Greek word translated *heed* is a compound word. It combines the Greek words translated "in" and "ear." We might translate it, "listen." This is the only place it is found in the entire New Testament which makes it very significant. It highlights the seriousness compelled by the Spirit to place the truth in the ears of those around Peter. They must understand and respond. Peter must pressure them with the truth of the indwelling Christ.

Let's review what has been discovered. In our text Luke states the tone and intensity of the situation (Acts 2:14). Peter is about to preach an explanation of what has taken place in the Pentecost event. What is the tone of his delivery? He is *standing* which is a verb in the passive voice. Peter is being acted upon by the Spirit through what has taken place in his life. He is drawn to his feet by the passion of the indwelling Christ. Also Peter *raised his* voice. This is deeper in meaning than simply shouting or becoming loud. It is the idea of "lifting up." God has elevated every thing in Christian experience to a new level. Peter's preaching must reflect this new elevation. Luke also reports that Peter *said* to them. This is a translation of a Greek word which is only used three times in the entire New Testament. All of them are in the Book of Acts. In the Old Testament (Septuagint) this is used only for wise and significant statements given by prophets or wise men. This is a message which is elevated beyond normal communication.

As Peter begins to speak he uses two phrases which set the tone for his message. He says, *"Let this be known to you."* The verb *be* is in the imperative mood. There is urgency for openness and understanding. He commands them to stretch to a new level of understanding. He continues by saying, *"Heed my words."* This is equivalent to "listen." It is a double statement of emphasis. Peter expresses the extreme importance of what is happening.

The atmosphere of the setting becomes very intense. This scene is elevated to a new level.

If that is not enough, Peter injects this same tone into the message as he preaches. The body of his message can be divided into three separate sections. Each section begins with a particular address or admonition (Acts 2:22, 29, 36). He begins his sermon with these words, *"Men of Israel, hear these words:"* (Acts 2:22). He urges them to recognize the sound waves coming from his lips. It is not the noise he wants them to hear. The Greek word has the idea of obedience. Jesus used this word at the close of several parables when He said, *"He who has ears to hear, let him hear!"* (Matthew 13:43). The emphasis of the Greek word is "come to know." There is urgency in his voice! He is desperate to communicate!

Peter introduces the second section of his message with another address. It is like calling out their personal names. He cries, *"Men and brethren, let me speak freely to you"* (Acts 2:29). This is a strange grammar construction in the Greek text. The actual main verb of the statement is **let me.** It is a translation of a Greek word which is composed of two very small words. The Greek words "ek" (from) and "eimi" (to be) are combined. Peter does not ask permission of the crowd. He says that the truth I am preaching to you is so great that it permits me to speak to you in this manner. The manner of my speaking is going to be *freely.* This is translated from two separate Greek words. The first means "among or amid." I am not going to do this behind your back but right in your face. The second word means "to express all that I am thinking." Something has captured me which I must reveal to you. I cannot hold back or soft pedal my words. I must forcibly

13

tell you the truth. The truth I have experienced demands a complete exposure. Christ in His fullness has come to indwell us. It is a new level which compels a complete openness on my part.

The third section of Peter's message begins, *"Therefore let all the house of Israel know assuredly that God has made this Jesus, whom you crucified, both Lord and Christ,"* (Acts 2:36). The main verb in his opening statement is *let...know.* It is translated from the Greek word "ginosko." It is in the imperative mood. Again we see the strong, commanding, urging emphasis. In the verse, he does not speak of grasping data. If he speaks of information he would use the Greek word "gnostos." If he is only interested in them understanding the concept he would use the Greek word "oida" for perceiving. What he desires is for them to enter into intimate relationship with Jesus who has become Lord and Christ. "Ginosko" is the Greek word for the most intimate relationship in marriage.

He also adds a very interesting word to this emphasis. It is translated *assuredly.* It comes from a word group which can be translated "certainty," "sure," or "to safeguard." The actual Greek word he uses in our text can be translated "securely." This actual Greek word is only used three times in the New Testament. Judas instructed the leaders of Israel in the capture of Jesus by saying, *"Whomever I kiss, He is the One; seize Him and lead Him away SAFELY,"* (Mark 14:44). Paul and Silas were in Philippi. There was a slave girl who was possessed with a spirit of divination. When Paul and Silas were used as instruments for her deliverance, the magistrates threw them in jail. They commanded *the jailer to keep them SECURELY* (Acts 16:23). As Peter is preaching after Pentecost, he says,

Therefore let all the house of Israel know ASSUREDLY that God has made this Jesus, whom you crucified, both Lord and Christ," (Acts 2:36). In this passage, Peter urges the people of Israel to be intimate with Jesus who is Lord and Christ for certain, securely, and absolutely. This has to be! They must enter into the embrace. The reality of who Jesus is must become their personal reality.

You cannot hear the tone clearly stated in the opening verse (Acts 2:14) without sensing a new intensity regarding the message. This is not a performance; there is no hidden agenda. The tone of the message is produced by the truth experienced. We have now experienced three different times within the message where Peter explodes with this same urgency. He is driven by the very reality of Christ who indwells him. He is captured by the resurrected Lord, the vision of the Kingdom, and now the indwelling Spirit. He burns with the truth! Everything has moved to a new level. The entrance level of the Old Testament has been replaced. The Spirit of Jesus within has superseded all they have experienced in commitment and relationship with Jesus in the flesh. Christ in you has become the new reality. This comes with a new level of intensity. Christ now consumes their lives.

How do you adequately express this? What should be the tone of your voice? Are you surprised I yell quite often? In our generation, one individual expressed it by crying out, "Take my life like a ten dollar bill and spend it all over town." He went on to express, "Let my life be like a candle which is lit on both ends until I am consumed for you." There is no room for a casual lukewarm attitude. Where does nominal Christianity fit into this picture? Christ has literally come to indwell the believer. The outside God has gotten inside. The dream and purpose of man has been filled. There is no room for yawning in this experience.

Whatever has duped us into the carefulness of man-invented strategies must be set aside. The author of the Book of Hebrews must have been yelling as he thundered into chapter twelve. *Therefore we also, since we are surrounded by so great a cloud of witnesses, let us lay aside every weight, and the sin which so easily ensnares us, and let us run with endurance the race that is set before us* (Hebrews 12:1). Every hindrance must be eliminated. We must not tolerate any element which might cause us to stumble. We must aggressively pour the reality of this message into our world. There is no time for strategy meetings. We must not soft pedal this message. We must compel every individual to embrace our Christ. We must fully enlist. We cannot delegate this to another. Senior adults cannot pass it to you. Teens must not think they can do it later. God calls us now!

2

God or the Devil?

ACTS 2:15

The Pentecost event has amazed the great crowd. The Jews of the Dispersion are astonished by the things they have seen. They have sought and longed for a new and fresh movement of God. Could this be the end of their search? They raise this issue (Acts 2:12), *"What ever could this mean?"* Then we see the Jews of Jerusalem. They see nothing to astonish them. They are stale and narrow, and they are quite satisfied with the way things are. Their opinion of the Pentecost event is *"They are full of new wine,"* (Acts 2:13).

Luke addresses the issue through the preaching of Peter. Before he actually presents the sermon, he sets the stage for us. He presents the TONE of the message first (Acts 2:14). The TRUTH of the message follows (Acts 2:15). It is a bold statement of correction before the proper explanation is given. Thirdly, he shares the TEXT of the message (Acts 2:16-21).

In this study we shall examine the TRUTH of the

message (Acts 2:15). Peter addresses both the Jews of the Dispersion and the Jews of Jerusalem in his overall message. The complete explanation of the Pentecost event (Acts 2:22-39) is focused on the Jews of the Dispersion. Their question is *"Whatever could this mean?"* (Acts 2:12). Peter goes to great lengths to satisfy their seeking. It is a detailed explanation of the movement of God on our behalf.

In our text (Acts 2:15), Peter directly answers the statement of the Jews of Jerusalem. They do not seek to embrace any new movement of God. They are ridgid and set in concrete. They explain the event away by saying, *"They are full of new wine,"* (Acts 2:13). It is a statement of mockery. Peter addresses their explanation. Their accusation is not worth more than one verse. Even if he gave more they would not listen. He simply says, *"For these are not drunk, as you suppose, since it is only the third hour of the day,"* (Acts 2:15). He gives them no deep spiritual insight. He does not reveal the unfolding plan of God. It is a simple statement of logic. He appeals to their intellect by saying how absurd their comment is. The third hour which is determined by sunrise is 9:00AM. Even those who are drunkards are not drunk this early in the day. This is especially true on a feast day such as Pentecost.

The key to understanding Peter's statement may be found in the Greek word translated *suppose.* This Greek word is only used five times in the entire New Testament and it is used in a variety of ways. It is used by Luke to describe the ascension of Christ (Acts 1:9). It is the word describing Jesus' response to a self-justifying lawyer who asks, *"And who is my neighbor?"* (Luke 10:29). It is a compound word meaning "under" and "to take." Its basic meaning is "to take from below." In our passage, there is a basic focus on the group that proposed this idea of drunkenness. The mockers have reached inside of themselves and proposed this idea. They do not seek beyond their own minds and hearts. They certainly are not open to a revelation from God regarding this matter. They explain everything from their own personal perspective. They do not seek an answer for what has happened. They already know the answer. If one is stuck in the mode of understanding everything within the framework of his own thinking, he is extremely limited.

When we limit ourselves to our own thinking, we most likely decide on a conclusion which is opposite of the real truth. That is the situation in our passage. The Jews of Jerusalem decide that the Pentecost event is a result of the devil. Drunkenness is considered by all Jews as obnoxious and sinful. Although drunkenness is common among the Greeks, it is a grievous accusation in Jewish Palestine. The Jews of Jerusalem view what God is doing as the work of the devil.

This is not the first time this has happened! They made this accusation enough times that they established a pattern. Consider the event recorded in Matthew 12:22-30. The fame of Jesus' miracles has spread over Palestine. On the occasion of a blind and mute man's healing *the multitudes were amazed* (Matthew 12:23). The man was actually demon possessed. A question spread through the members of the crowd. *"Could this be the Son of David?"* they asked (Matthew 12:23). The very suggestion that Jesus might be the Messiah is a threat to the authority of the Pharisees. They immediately attempt to make their conclusion that of the multitude. They say, *"This fellow does not cast out demons except by Beelzebub, the ruler of the demons,"* (Matthew 12:24). Again they attribute God's actions to the devil.

An amazing discourse results from their accusation. The initial response parallels our passage in the Book of Acts (2:15). Jesus approaches them on the level of logic (Matthew 12:25-30). What they say does not make any sense! How can they possibly come to this conclusion? They are educated and intelligent individuals. Their conclusion is a result of limiting their thinking to their own understanding. Self-centeredness dominates and determines all of their conclusions. To step outside of their self-centered thinking would be to risk being influenced by something beyond them.

They have not realized how destructive it is to approach everything in one's life from a self-centered view. It is simply the devil casting out his own demons which means he is *divided against himself* (Matthew 12:26). But this is the way self-centeredness acts. It will do anything to make itself look good. Self-centeredness is so focused on self that it cannot see the destruction brought about by its own actions.

This is what happens when a man thinks only of himself in his marriage and family. He gets married because he sincerely wants love and companionship. He desires a home, family and intimacy. But his self-centeredness demands its own way. He takes advantage of his wife. His lack of patience causes him to abuse his children in the discipline process. He spills a spirit of rebellion and death into his home. He builds barriers in his relationships. He destroys everything good in the home he sincerely wanted.

The same is true in the local body of Christ. All church members want the movement of God. There is a desire for revival and evangelism. Many individuals began attending because of their desire for love and fellowship. However, an attachment to tradition caused by self-centeredness brings division. Disagreements flourish and kill the Spirit of revival and evangelism. Love and fellowship give way to hatred and war. Self-centeredness destroys everything originally desired. It is the devil casting out his own demons.

This kind of situation is so serious that Jesus says it cannot be forgiven (Matthew 12:31-37). It is called "the blasphemy against the Holy Spirit." Jesus is very clear about the content of the unforgivable sin. It is not a deed or action, but it is spirit and attitude. Jesus is very forgiving to sinners, but He cannot and will not tolerate people with unholy attitudes. These people are not open and seeking. They are hypocrites focused on themselves, and they destroy everything around them in an attempt to save themselves. In reality, they attribute to the devil the very works of God.

The group gathered at the crucifixion of Christ expressed this same attitude. Jesus and the leaders of Israel were at extreme odds over the cross style. The "pour your life out" concept is foreign to the "grab for yourself" style. They did not just misunderstand the cross style but it greatly irritated them. They could not leave Jesus alone. His style was a threat to all they stood for! In their typical self-centered style they worked diligently to eliminate Him. Cross style deserves to be nailed to a cross. The deed is done (Matthew 27:35).

Even then they cannot help but express their

bewilderment. They are again mocking Him as He pours out His life for others. The leadership of Israel (chief priests, scribes and elders) are yelling, *"He saved others; Himself He cannot save. If He is the King of Israel, let Him now come down from the cross, and we will believe Him. He trusted in God; let Him deliver Him now if He will have Him; for He said, 'I am the Son of God,'"* (Matthew 27:42-43). What a concept! They give expression to their very self-centered nature. They cannot conceive how anyone in intimacy with God can possibly be subjected to such a death as crucifixion. If Jesus really is the King of Israel, God will surely protect Him from such shame. If Jesus is truly the Son of God and doing the very works of God, will not God intervene on His behalf now? Therefore, if He has not been doing the work of God, indeed, He must be doing the work of the devil. So the cross is simply the climax or result of the work of the devil in the life of Christ.

Do you see the clear expression of their self-centeredness? If the leaders of Israel are intimate with God and are placed in such a circumstance, their self-centeredness will immediately use the power of God for their personal deliverance. They cannot possibly understand why Jesus does not do the same. God's activity in pouring out your life for others is totally foreign to their thinking. Thus, they ultimately attribute the crucifixion to demonic activity in the life of Christ when all the time God has planned it. They are again attributing the works of God to the devil.

But the pattern continues! The soldiers who are the elite of the Roman forces are guarding the dead body of Jesus. A Roman seal has been placed on the tomb. No one can possibly steal the body of Christ and propose the ridiculous conclusion of resurrection. However, God acts again. An angel of the Lord descends bringing a revelation of the resurrection. The fiercest of the Roman soldiers faint from fright. Upon reviving, they immediately run into Jerusalem to report the event to the leaders of Israel. It is one more of God's attempts to offer an opportunity of grace to these Jews. The soldiers *reported to the chief priests all the things that had happened* (Matthew 28:11).

The response of the chief priests is predictable for they follow the same pattern. *When they had assembled with the elders and consulted together, they gave a large sum of money to the soldiers, saying, "Tell them, 'His disciples came at night and stole Him away while we slept,'"* (Matthew 28:12). The key to their response is the Greek word translated *consulted together.* In the noun form it is translated "council." It paints the picture of a group of men sitting around the table discussing what they know. They turn into themselves for the answer to their dilemma. Out of their self-centeredness the decision is made.

They decide the disciples have stolen the body or at least that is their proposal. Stealing is of the devil. Therefore, the resurrection of Christ which is definitely the act of God is now being attributed to the devil. The source of this conclusion is their self-centered consulting. They constantly manipulate the people involved with their conclusions. *So they took the money and did as they were instructed; and this saying is commonly reported among the Jews until this day* (Matthew 26:15).

We need to ask and answer a series of questions for our personal lives! "How do we do this in our lives?" I want you to think carefully about those things against which you have taken issue. Do you have strong Biblical basis for your resistance or is it simply personal preference? My mind immediately rushes to many circumstances which have caused divisions in churches. I have experienced arguments and conflict over furnaces, communion tables, music and where the pulpit is placed. In one church great division arose over five gallon buckets of sand. Some caring people of the church were ministering to several homeless people from downtown. The homeless always needed to go outside between Sunday school and church to smoke. Those caring for these people had provided several buckets of sand at the front door of the building for the deposit of the remains of the cigarettes. The following Sunday morning the buckets were gone. They were found behind the building. Each time they were moved to the front of the building they would later turn up missing. Some folks did not want buckets of sand filled with cigarette butts in front of the church doors. Is this not attributing to the devil the works of God? Self-centeredness will not allow the individual to recognize that God is doing a new thing in the lives of people. It is easy to become so attached to tradition and self-centered patterns we find ourselves fighting against God. We attribute any deviation from our tradition to the work of the devil. What if God attempts to do a new thing as He did at Pentecost?

A second question needs to be answered. "How serious is this issue?" Surely the impact of the truth discovered answers this question for us. When the Pharisees criticize Jesus for linking with the devil (Matthew 12:24), they shut the door to any activity of God in their lives. If we attribute what God is doing to the devil, there will never be any positive response to God's action in our lives. How will we ever receive any new instruction from God? Time and again Christ desperately attempts to communicate the truth to the leaders of Israel, even through the pagan soldiers at the resurrection, but they will not listen. They will not recognize the moving hand of God in the events which are shattering their traditions. Thus, they attribute to the devil the works of God.

There is a third question of importance. "How can I tell if it is God's action or that of the devil?" Did you notice in each of the Biblical illustrations above, it is self-centeredness which sources the confusion? You can never distinguish between God's action and the devil's without a complete death to self-centeredness. Those who seek and respond do not seem to have a problem. It is in openness we hear His voice and recognize His actions. The heart which seeks sincerely cannot miss His will. He will not allow that individual to be confused. This is a startling and comforting truth to one as ignorant as me.

Now we are confronted by a fourth question. "Can God use an event for His purpose which He did not cause?" Perhaps the devil causes an event and yet God utilizes this circumstance for His own will. Therefore, to fight against the circumstance caused by the devil would be to hinder the purpose of God. A powerful example of this is stated in the preaching of Peter in response to Pentecost. Peter says, *"Him* (Christ), *being delivered by the determined purpose and foreknowledge of God, you have taken by lawless hands, have crucified, and put to death,"* (Acts 2:23). We must understand the depth of this truth. There seems to be two views of the crucifixion. There is the perspective of the men who think they are in charge. They plot in secret meetings to bring about the crucifixion. Their lawless hands do the work of the devil. Therefore the crucifixion is the result of the devil's action. But there is a second view. Christ is delivered by the determined purpose and foreknowledge of God. God is so sovereign and omniscient that He calculated into His plan the lawless deeds of men. He is so redemptive He changed what was intended to be bad into good. Jesus surrendered to what looked like the acts of the devil, because He knew it was the plan of God. Redemption was the result!

Can I be open and intimate with Christ? Can I know His heart and grasp His intent? Can I receive His mind until I know His thoughts? Can I live in every circumstance finding His will? Can His purpose be accomplished through me in all the confused circumstances of my day? Is this not His plan???

3

PETER'S EXPLANATION

ACTS 2:16-39

The Pentecost event has taken place (Acts 2:1-4). The earth shaking reality of this happening is equal to everything God has accomplished up to this point. Everything is changed! No one can ever be the same again. The Jews of the Dispersion are completely awestruck. Luke highlights it five different times (Acts 2:6, 7, and 12). The Jews of Jerusalem react in their normal stale manner. They even slip into mockery (Acts 2:13). The entire movement of God is dismissed as they proclaim, *"They are full of new wine."* A proper explanation is desperately needed. The Jews of the Dispersion seek while the Jews of Jerusalem seclude themselves. The record must be set straight. Peter is on his feet. The Holy Spirit gives an amazing explanation with startling results.

Luke presents this explanation by making a contrast between man's view and God's view. The mockers have just had their say. It is puny, meager, and mechanical. Even a casual glance reveals how illogical it is. However, it is the best the reasoning of man can produce. God acts and men interpret it through the filter of their own minds. They are incredibly far from the truth. The huge dreams of God are reduced down to the understanding of man. But isn't this what God has faced year after year throughout the Old Testament? People with such limited capacities refuse to rely on the wisdom of God. Man, who was built to be an instrument of the movement of God, requires God to become a tool of his own designs. The best we can calculate is illogical. We even label the works of God as the actions of the devil.

BUT there is much more to it than this! God is acting. The dream of God for mankind is restored. What God intended in the creation of man was lost in sin but is now corrected. God has come to indwell man again. Everything which kept that from happening is made right. This is the crowning segment of man's redemption. God's step by step plan is accomplished. The devil views this Pentecost movement as deserving of only one simple statement; BUT God sees it as worthy of over one half of the chapter. The devil responds only by mocking; BUT God proposes the glory of mankind's restoration. The devil easily dismisses the event; BUT God must focus us on the reality of being filled with the Spirit of Jesus.

While the mockers dismiss the Pentecost event with a few words of mockery (Acts 2:13), Peter is on his feet (Acts 2:14). He spends only one sentence correcting the mockers (Acts 2:15) and then quickly moves into a full-blown explanation of the greatness of what God has just accomplished. He preaches a powerful sermon which greatly convicts the Jews of the Dispersion. Three thousand of them become Christians (Acts 2:41).

It is important that we view the sermon as a whole. The entire discourse is thoroughly saturated with Scripture. He simply refers to the Old Testament. These Jews are committed to the Scriptures. Peter thunders the news that the Old Testament Scriptures verify what God is doing. He begins with a Scriptural basis which was spoken by the prophet Joel (Acts 2:17-21). He then gives a three-verse explanation (Acts 2:22-24) which is based on a quotation from King David (Acts 2:25-28). Peter continues with more insight (Acts 2:29-33) based on a second quotation from King David (Acts 2:34-35). A definite progression dominates his message.

Peter begins with a strong quotation from the prophet Joel (Acts 2:17-21). In this passage from Joel, he captures the very heart of the Pentecost event. It is a quotation from Joel 2:28-32. We will deal with the details of this prophecy and its fulfillment in a later study. In our overall view, the important thing is to grasp the central theme of the prophecy. The resounding theme is given to us twice:

"That I will pour out My Spirit on all flesh..." (Acts 2:17).

"I will pour out My Spirit in those days..." (Acts 2:18).

Everything else in the passage has to do with the result of this great outpouring. Therefore, Peter's message boldly states that this prophecy has just been fulfilled in their presence. They have just experienced the action of God. He takes His very nature and plants it in the human life of mankind. Obviously the results of this action will take man to a new level of living. This was to take place in *the last days* (Acts 2:17). Peter boldly says, "The *last days* have arrived!" The emphasis of these *last days* is not judgment (although that may be present). It is not about church growth. The Spirit of Jesus is being poured out on the believers. Everything God has been working towards throughout the Old Testament has come to pass in this moment.

As Peter begins this message (Acts 2:22), he proclaims, "Let me share with you how we finally got here! It all happened through one man. He was not just a man. He was a man who made Himself totally available to God so God could do something through Him." Let us look at his sermon.

DOCTRINE OF THE INCARNATION
Acts 2:24
The actions of God are taking place in Christ

The first three verses of his sermon (Acts 2:22-24) are the explanation of the Scripture he quotes from King David (Acts 2:25-28). Notice this very important fact! He never says that Jesus is Divine. This is not a result of disbelief in Christ. Certainly his belief is well established in his confession. *Simon Peter answered and said, "You are the Christ, the Son of the living God,"* (Matthew 16:16). But this is not his emphasis. Is this not a surprise? Would it not have been proper to cry out that the Divine Son of God has accomplished this? The very One they crucified was God!

However, Peter's emphasis is on what God is doing through this Man called Christ. Look at the strong statements in his sermon:

"Men of Israel, hear these words: Jesus of Nazareth, a Man attested by God to you by miracles, wonders, and signs which God did through Him in your midst,

as you yourselves also know..." (Acts 2:22).

"Him, being delivered by the determined purpose and foreknowledge of God..." (Acts 2:23).

"Whom God raised up, having loosed the pains of death..." (Acts 2:24).

This is a strong proclamation of the Doctrine of Incarnation. "Incarnation" means "to assume flesh." "The Doctrine of the Incarnation" means that the second member of the Trinity leaped from His throne to assume the body and nature of mankind. In one person, there was the total nature of God and the total nature of man in an indissoluble union. "Indissoluble" means you cannot split Him into parts. He is not half-God and half-man. He does not sometimes act as God and other times as man. In order for Him to become man, He was required to set aside those things He had as God. Everything which distinguished Him from man was set aside. Here was a man who totally responded to God for His moment by moment life.

The life of Christ is not explained in the fact that He is God, although we all believe that is true. His life is explained in the fact that He was a man filled with God. Jesus lived like He could not live through the power of the Holy Spirit. The miracles, wonders, and signs which He accomplished were only because God did them *through Him* (Acts 2:22). Even the tragic evil which appeared to be the result of *lawless hands, have crucified, and put to death* were really the *determined purpose and foreknowledge of God* (Acts 2:23). God simply would not allow Jesus to remain in death, but *God raised up* (Acts 2:24). If you desire to know how an individual lives when he is filled with God and constantly responds to God, Jesus is the answer.

The *last days* have now arrived! The prophecy of Joel is now fulfilled. How did we get here? It is through this Man called Christ, who though He is God, submitted to the incarnation. God became man and set aside everything which distinguished Him from man. He lived in total response to God. This is what enabled His crucifixion and resurrection to bring us to this moment. Without this we would still be under the Old Covenant with nothing but our performance and law. It is a new hour because of this Man called Christ! Peter bases this truth on the statement of King David (Acts 2:25-28).

DIRECTION OF THE INCARNATION
Acts 2:29-33
The unfolding plans of God are taking place in Christ

The second point in Peter's sermon highlights the long range plans of God which are based on promises God made to King David (Acts 2:29-33). It was during a time of victory for King David and Israel. The Ark of the Covenant had just been returned to Jerusalem. David and the people were rejoicing with such delight. The Scripture says, **Then David danced before the Lord with all his might;** (2 Samuel 6:14). Through the prophet Nathan a message was given to King David. A key element in that message was this promise: *"Also the Lord tells you that He will make you a house. When your days are fulfilled and you rest with your fathers, I will set up your seed after you, who will come from your body, and I will establish his kingdom. He shall build a house for My name, and I will establish the throne of his kingdom*

32

forever... And your house and your kingdom shall be established forever before you. Your throne shall be established forever," (2 Samuel 7:11-13, 16).

It is indeed true that King David is *both dead and buried, and his tomb is with us to this day* (Acts 2:29). But *God had sworn with an oath to him* (Acts 2:30). This promise was centered in the coming Messiah. The throne of King David was to be protected by God. It would never disappear, but God would raise up from the seed of King David One who would reign on that throne forever and ever. King David, as a prophet, foresaw this (Acts 2:31). In Psalms sixteen he spoke concerning the resurrection of Christ from the dead. God would not allow *His soul... left in Hades, nor did His flesh see corruption* (Acts 2:31). God simply intervened in the life and death of this Man called Jesus. *This Jesus God has raised up* (Acts 2:32). He was exalted to the right hand of God for the purpose of receiving the promise of the Holy Spirit. Due to these facts, we are now experiencing the very event which is being questioned! He has *poured out this which you now see and hear* (Acts 2:33).

Has this not been the plan of God from the very first disobedience of man? Did God not begin a restoration plan from the very beginning of sin? Is this not the fulfillment of the dreams of God for mankind? Is it not all found in the Christ who has provided the indwelling Spirit? King David was not the fulfillment of this. He is dead, buried, and certainly did not ascend into the heavens (Acts 2:34). But Christ, from the seed of David, has ascended. David saw it as a prophet and rejoiced in its truth. All of this has happened through the Man called Christ.

What is happening in the great Pentecost event has been the long range dream of God for us. To actually see the event and label it as a result of drunkenness is to reject God's long range plan. We must open ourselves to the indwelling of the Spirit as Christ did. As God moved through the Christ, He now wants to move through us. As Christ experienced the fulfillment of the dreams of God within His own person, so we must embrace the same fulfillment within us.

DREAM OF THE INCARNATION
Acts 2:36-39
What is taking place in Jesus is for you

Peter thunders to the close of his explanation to the Jews. It is a conclusion which includes them. God has plans and dreams for His world. Instead of allowing these to be fulfilled, the Jews attempt to destroy them (Acts 2:36). They fought against all that God is accomplishing. But God is greater than their feeble attempts. *"God has made this Jesus, whom you crucified, both Lord and Christ"* (Acts 2:36). They join forces with the enemy. They, who were chosen to be an avenue of mercy, become a blockade of defiance. When this truth dawns on them they are shocked. *Now when they heard this, they were cut to the heart* (Acts 2:37). They cry out from the depths of their hearts for instruction in how to respond. They groan, *"Men and brethren, what shall we do?"* (Acts 2:37). How can we make this right? How can we undo what we have done? What can we do now that will make up for what we have done? We have crucified Christ!

The answer is clear! There is nothing you can do. No act or actions can set this right! The fact is there is a *"promise... to you and to your children, and to all who are afar off, as many as the Lord our God will call,"* (Acts 2:39). Will you respond to God at this moment? He is calling you now. It is a call to *Repent* (Acts 2:38). Give up a former thought and embrace a second thought. Please change your mind. You have lived in the attitude of crucifying Christ, but now you see a new truth. Will you abandon the former thought for the sake of the new which God has so graciously provided you? It is the baptism that John the Baptist called you to a few years ago (Matthew 3). This very act of responding ushers in the forgiveness which God has already provided. You cannot make what you have done right. There are not enough religious deeds, regardless of how sacrificial, which can atone for your rejection of Christ who is the fulfilled dream of God. Will you in humility simply respond to what God is showing you now? If so, you will be forgiven and you will receive the *gift of the Holy Spirit* (Acts 2:38), the event which attracted your attention.

What God has done through the Man called Christ, He wants to do through you. All the fullness of God contained in Christ can now be in you. The God who acted through Christ now wants to act through you. That which attracted you to Jesus is a result of the Spirit of God. He is now yours as well! This is God's plan, embrace it!

4

THE TEXT OF PENTECOST

ACTS 2:16-21

The ten tribes of Israel have been taken into exile
never to return. The southern kingdom of Judah
remains. However, Judah has not continued faithful
to God. A sudden disaster falls without warning. An
awe-striking black cloud descends upon the land. It is
the dreaded locusts. In a matter of hours, every living
green thing has been stripped bare. Did not God allow
this to happen because of their sin? The prophet Joel,
God's spokesman for that hour, rises to the occasion. His
book, while only a brief three chapters is powerful in its
impact. He contends that the judgments of God during
the Day of the Lord will be far worse than the plague of
the locusts. This disaster is a mere call to awaken and
respond in repentance.

While there is a strong emphasis on God's inability
to tolerate sin, the blessings which are to come are
unparalleled. Peter highlights this section of Joel's
prophecy as fulfilled (Acts 2:16-21). It becomes the text

for his message which explains the event of the filling of the Holy Spirit which they just experienced. The focus of his quote from the Book of Joel is:

That I will pour out my Spirit upon all flesh... (Acts 2:17).

I will pour out My Spirit in those days... (Acts 2:18).

Everything in prophecy described by Joel is a result of this generous outpouring of the Spirit of God. There will be ***prophesy, visions,*** and ***dreams*** which all point to the sourcing of the Spirit of Christ. Even the ***wonders in heaven above and the signs in the earth beneath*** are a product of this new movement of God within the life of mankind.

The focus is not on God's final judgment of the world, although that may be mentioned. It is not on the final damnation of those who have rebelled against God, although that is certainly true. The entire prophecy is about the indwelling of God within the life of man. Joel is speaking about Pentecost! This results in salvation. In the prophecy there is a sense of completeness, of arrival. Pentecost is the final piece of the puzzle. It is the last nail driven into the board. The dream of God is fulfilled!

At first glance, one might think we have moved from a focus on Christ to a focus on the Holy Spirit. Peter completely corrects this in his message. We have arrived at this moment of the outpouring of the Spirit of God because of Christ. Christ became man and dwelt among us. Christ became an avenue for the great miracles of God (Acts 2:22). Christ, in submission to the Father, experienced the cross (Acts 2:23). Christ was raised from the dead by God (Acts 2:24). Christ was ***exalted to the right hand of God*** (Acts 2:33). He ***received from*** *the Father the promise of the Holy Spirit* (Acts 2:33). It is Christ who *poured out this which you now see and hear* (Acts 2:33). The only way any individual can enter into oneness with God is through Christ (Acts 2:38). We know the very Spirit an individual receives is the Spirit of Christ!

As we view the structure of the prophecy of Joel quoted by Peter, there are some definite aspects to this focus on the filling of the Holy Spirit. Let me list them for you.

PERIOD OF TIME

Peter begins his quotation from Joel by saying, *And it shall come to pass in the last days, says God, that I will pour out my Spirit on all flesh* (Acts 2:17).

If this is compared carefully with the actual Book of Joel, you will find Peter does not quote it correctly. The Prophet Joel said: *And it shall come to pass afterward that I will pour out My Spirit on all flesh* (Joel 2:28).

Peter changed the words to emphasize when this prophecy will take place. Joel says it is *afterward;* Peter says it is *in the last days.* This is not accidental or from a lack of memory. Peter interprets Joel's statement and applies it to his (and our) hour. Joel states this event will take place in the future, while Peter describes the present time period in which the Spirit of God comes in His fullness.

This phrase (*the last days*) is not unusual even in the Old Testament. The prophet Isaiah used it (Isaiah 2:2). The prophet Micah also used it (Micah 4:1). In both cases they refer to the time of the Messiah. The author of the Book of Hebrews introduces "God's Superior Revelation" to us by contrasting God's message, which came through the prophets, with the fact that God *has in these last days spoken to us by His Son, whom He has appointed heir of all things, through whom also He made the worlds;* (Hebrews 1:2).

In the coming of Christ the ancient economy was closed and a new, superior economy appeared. The *last days* signified the terminating of all the preparatory arrangements. We are no longer getting ready for anything since Christ has come! This was the emphasis John the Baptist preached. *"Repent, for the kingdom of heaven is at hand!"* (Matthew 3:2). The King of the Kingdom has arrived. The waiting period is over; Christ is here!

We are living in those days. All God wants to do within us is now available. Everything He has planned for you is at your finger tips. We do not need to wait for God to do anything else. It is all in place. These are the *last days.* We are living in the fullness of the Spirit. The prophets of old longed to experience and only saw by faith these *last days.* What a privileged people we are! There is no reason for us to live in defeat, confusion, or discouragement. Do not tolerate compromise! I am deeply concerned about an evangelical Christianity which wants to abide in an anemic, subnormal existence. The excuse is given that the final judgment has not come. We are still in the flesh. Therefore, we do not experience all God wants to do in us. This is not the emphasis of the New Testament. These are the *last days.* God has completed the work through Christ. Everything we need to be in intimacy with Him is now ours. There is nothing to stop us from experiencing the nature of God. We can be His! The thrust of this truth is that this is for you. You qualify! You are in the *last days.*

PRESENTATION

Another strong emphasis in the prophecy of Joel is the picture of *pour out.* It is interesting that Joel would use these words to express the coming of the Holy Spirit. This phrase is not new to us in the New Testament. Jesus spoke to His disciples concerning fasting. He used the illustration of the new wine in old wineskins. New wine will cause old wineskins to break and *the wine is spilled* (Matthew 9:17). The Greek word translated *spilled* is the same as *pour out.* The picture is one of being completely emptied, spilling, or gushing.

Paul gives testimony to his past actions regarding the persecution of Christians. He admits to Christ, *"And when the blood of Your martyr Stephen was shed, I also was standing by consenting to his death, and guarding the clothes of those who were killing him,"* (Acts 22:20). The Greek word translated *was shed* is the same as *pour out.*

Luke gives us some additional information about the end of Judas' life (Acts 1:18). He tried to hang himself by tying a rope around a tree which was near a precipice. Evidently the rope broke *and falling headlong, he burst open in the middle and all of his entrails gushed out* (Acts 1:18). The Greek word translated *gushed out* is the same as *pour out.*

The definition of the word goes beyond the idea of simply "coming out." It carries with it the concept of abundance or lavished. It is the picture of a full bucket turned upside down. There is no holding back. There are no restrictions. Peter not only quotes this word in the prophecy of Joel, but also adopts it as his own description of the coming of the Holy Spirit. In the climax of his sermon, he says, *"Therefore being exalted to the right hand of God, and having received from the Father the promise of the Holy Spirit, He poured out this which you now see and hear,"* (Acts 2:33).

Christ has received the promise of the Father. He has not given His Spirit to us in meager portions. He has not restricted the gift of His Spirit. He is not bargaining with us about His presence. You CANNOT have as much of God as you want. You cannot choose a little or a lot. He will not give Himself in portions. He is extravagantly, lavishly, abundantly, without hesitation or restrictions giving Himself to us. The intent is that He will fill our entire being or not at all. All areas of our lives will be filled with His presence or we will not know Him. What a promise we have received! The thrust of this truth is that this is for you. You qualify! There is the fullness of God for you in the abundance of the outpouring of the Spirit of Christ. This truth is also demonstrated in the next great aspect of our text.

PEOPLE INVOLVED

When Joel used the Greek word translated *pour out,* he was contrasting the present coming of the Spirit of Christ with the few appearances of the Holy Spirit in the Old Testament. He continues with a similar contrast by saying, *"I will pour out my Spirit upon all flesh;"* (Acts 2:17). This presents a contrast with the restriction of the Spirit of Christ to certain privileged people throughout the Old Testament. He goes on to interpret his own prophecy in great detail. He gives us a list of those who are included in *all flesh.*

In the New Testament the Greek word translated *all* is used well over one thousand times. It is very important to know if an article is placed before the word. When an article is used it limits the word to a focused meaning. It focuses on a group and everyone within that group. However, when there is no article it emphasizes the broadest sense of the word. In our passage there is no article before the word! Joel is saying and Peter emphasizes the greatest view of the outpouring of the Holy Spirit. Also, this Greek word includes the idea of oneness, a totality or the whole.

As God speaks through the prophet Joel, He interprets His own prophecy with a list. The significance of the list seems to be found in the removal of all distinctions. There is no sexual distinction. *Your sons and your daughters shall prophecy.* The age distinction is quickly discarded. *Your young men shall see vision, Your old men shall dream dreams.* Even the status distinction is removed. *And on My menservants and on My maidservants.*

While these are the distinctions specifically mentioned in the prophecy, there are other divisions which are implied. There are no racial distinctions. Think of the strong division between Jew and Gentile in the cultural environment of the New Testament. However, Paul cries out, *For you are all sons of God through faith in Christ Jesus. For as many of you as were baptized into Christ have put on Christ. There is neither Jew nor Greek, there is neither slave nor free, there is neither male nor female; for you are all one in Christ Jesus* (Galatians 3:26:28).

There are no educational distinctions. This is highlighted by the leaders of Israel gathered together to confront the apostles. Peter's reasoning and clarity is so powerful, they are amazed. *Now when they saw the boldness of Peter and John, and perceived that they were uneducated and untrained men, they marveled* (Acts 4:13).

The list goes on and on. There are no distinctions between personality types. Isn't it significant that this distinction is never highlighted? There is no past distinction. People who have committed sins in the past are not excluded; all are included. Even those who had been their enemies and responsible for the deaths of their companions (Saul of Tarsus) were included! There is no talent distinction. One cannot discover in the Book of Acts a prayer for God to foster certain talents in the church. Even when the apostles were searching for those who could "serve tables," they desired *seven men of good reputation, full of the Holy Spirit and wisdom...* (Acts 6:3). It was spiritual qualities they desired, not talent.

There was no prosperity distinction. Regardless of their personal economy status, they were included. It is simply never mentioned as an issue. There was no tenured distinction. From the very first recorded business meeting of the early church they were all included (Acts 1:15). The brothers of Christ who were converted during the cross event were included in the decisions as were the apostles who had been with Jesus the entire time of His earthly ministry.

Why are we so prone to distinctions? We seem to pride ourselves in our differences. In our attitudes we foster the "haves" and the "have nots." We applaud the performance, the accomplishments of those with talent. Is it not an expression of our self-centered carnality?

44

Something wonderful has taken place among the disciples. Jesus has become so dominant that nothing else matters. Christianity became totally about Jesus, not about the disciples and their distinctions.

The wonder of this truth is that you qualify. Everything God wants you to have is now here. There is nothing to hold you back. We are in *the last days.* The final piece of the puzzle has been put in place. Christ has accomplished all! He is everything God has dreamed for us. Concerning the distinction between Jews and Gentiles, Paul says, *For He Himself is our peace, who has made both one, and has broken down the middle wall of separation, having abolished in His flesh the enmity, that is, the law of commandments contained in ordinances, so as to create in Himself one new man from the two, thus making peace* (Ephesians 2:14-15). Outside of Christ, there are distinctions. Outside of Christ, we battle for position and make ourselves superior to others. But these are *the last days.* We are now in Christ and Christ is now in us! Regardless of all man-made distinctions, we are included.

PURPOSE

But there is one last aspect in our text. We have mentioned the idea of "arrival." We are in *the last days.* This is where God has been going throughout the entire Old Testament. Everything is now done. We have arrived! However, this is not in the sense "over." It is not that we now know it all. It is arrival in the sense of all that God wants us to have is now available to us. We have come to a new level in Christ. There is now going to be an accelerated revelation. Joel prophesied this; Peter proposed it.

In the outpouring of the Spirit of Christ came *prophecy, visions, dreams, wonders,* and *signs.* Is it not interesting that he did not mention prosperity, health, and happiness? His list is focused on the expanded revelation of Christ. But this should not surprise us for John told us this in his Gospel account. John records the statement of Jesus, *"However, when He, the Spirit of truth, has come, He will guide you into all truth; for He will not speak on His own authority, but whatever He hears He will speak; and He will tell you things to come,"* (John 16:13). There is going to be an accelerated revelation of the truth. Jesus said, *"I am the way, the truth, and the life,"* (John 14:6). This is not an academic pursuit, but a spiritual revelation. This will not be given to a few as in the Old Testament, but all distinctions are broken down in the New Covenant.

You qualify! We are in *the last days.* Everything is yours because Christ is yours. Would you embrace His Spirit? Would you be embraced by His Spirit?

5

THE PROOF

ACTS 2:22

On the Feast Day of Pentecost God restored to mankind the intimacy of His presence. It was the climax of His dreams for mankind and His purpose throughout the Old and New Testaments. The beginning was small. Only one hundred and twenty experienced His fullness at the start. What happened was so powerful it demanded explanation. Peter, moved by the Holy Spirit, stands to preach the revelation of God. He presents his text from the prophecy of Joel and then moves into his sermon.

Peter proclaims three verses of revelation and then supports it with a quotation from David (Psalms 16:8-11). The grammar structure of these three verses is significant (Acts 2:22-24). The opening statement of the verses presents to us a simple statement. *"Men of Israel, hear these words;"* (Acts 2:22). Then the rest of the three verses is one long sentence. It is somewhat complicated by its length; thus it can be confusing. The main subject of the sentence is a reflective pronoun which can be translated "self." It is "self" in all persons such as myself, yourself, or himself. It is used for emphasis. It sets the

47

individual apart from everything else. It is therefore translated in our passage as *you yourselves* (Acts 2:22). This is not a general statement about the people of the world. Peter addresses the Jews who are in the temple area. They have surrounded the hundred and twenty who have just experienced Pentecost. What Peter says applies directly to them.

The main verb of the sentence is *know* (Acts 2:22). The English word *know* is a translation of the Greek word "oida." It means "to see, perceive, or apprehend." It can have the idea of physically seeing, but goes much deeper than sight. It is an inward grasping and understanding of the happening being perceived. This concept becomes the major thrust of Peter's message. He is not proposing new information to them or uncovering a hidden doctrine. It is not impossible for the Jews to see the truth though they are possessed by their tradition. They still have a chance. Peter literally says to them, "I am only telling you what you already know and understand! The only way this truth can confuse you is for you to choose confusion. You refuse to know!"

The same is true for us. What I do not know is not a problem for me. Herein lays my difficulty. I do know and refuse to obey. The thundering message of "prevenient grace" is light. This has come to all of us. He reveals Himself to everyone. Have we responded to His revelation? Are we walking in all of the light we have received? The message of Peter is only a presentation of what we already know and understand.

What is this revelation already revealed? It is the revelation of the person of *Jesus of Nazareth.* Peter opens with a short sentence, and the very first words of his lengthy sentence is *Jesus of Nazareth.* It is in the accusative case. This means it acts like a direct object which receives the action of the verb. Since the main verb is *know,* Jesus becomes the focus of that action. The revelation of God is focused in this Person. If anything is clearly understood and seen of God, it is through this Person. The only possible avenue of insight into God is through Jesus. I am not speaking of a vision or dream which came to a special prophet. This is not what someone has told us they think they may have seen. This is not the opinion of a small group of people attempting to lure others. This is about *Jesus of Nazareth.*

Peter does not present Jesus as "Jesus, the Son of God," though He certainly is that Person. He is not portrayed as the second member of the Triune Godhead, although this too is true. He is *Jesus of Nazareth.* He is literally "Jesus, the Nazarene." He is one of us. He has a birth certificate and a grandfather. A city of vile reputation is His hometown. Upon hearing Jesus was from Nazareth, Nathanael said, *"Can anything good come out of Nazareth?"* (John 1:46). He does not come to us as One from the highest, but One from the lowest. We do not see Him as One well connected, but One who is alone.

The very next words in the Greek text follow the English translation. They are *a Man.* This is translated from one Greek word which is also in the accusative case. This means it is a direct object also. These Jews not only know *Jesus of Nazareth,* but they also know He was *a Man.* They experienced the miracles of Jesus. They heard His teachings. They were a part of the group responsible for the crucifixion of Christ (Acts 2:36-37).

Jesus was not an historical figure about whom they read. He certainly was not an angel who appeared and disappeared from among them at various times. He was not the resurrected form of an Old Testament prophet, and He was not a ghost. Jesus was a literal, actual man! This crowd of Jews embraced Him as such. All of their conversations spoke of Him as *a Man*. Even the leadership of Israel dealt with Him as *a Man.*

While there were certainly a variety of aspects concerning the presence of *Jesus of Nazareth, a Man,* there is only one thing which we must consider according to the text (Acts 2:22)! He is *a Man attested by God to you* (Acts 2:22). This statement forms an accusative phrase which receives the action of the main verb, *know.* The Greek word translated *attested* is actually a participle. In this case, it acts like an adjective giving content to *a Man.* It becomes clear that whatever is going on in this *Man* called Jesus, it is coming from God. The Greek word translated *by* is "apo." Its primary translation is "from." It basically means the going forth or proceeding of one object from another. In this case, the attesting is coming from God, the Father.

The Greek word translated *to* is "eis." It has the primary idea of motion into any place or thing. It is normally translated "in" or "into." First of all there is the action of what you already know and have experienced. This action is acting upon this *Man* called Jesus. He is an individual who is *attested.* This actually comes through or from the person of God. It is so personal that God has brought this to you as an individual. There is no way to say, "I did not know." This is not over your head. God has revealed it personally to you. You know!

The entire thrust of this idea seems to depend upon the word *attested.* It is for that reason we must thoroughly grasp its meaning and significance. The basic Greek word means "to show or display." The Greek word in our text has "apo" as a prefix. This gives it the idea of coming from someone or something. This Greek verb only occurs four times in the New Testament. These four times give us the various usages of the word. Paul said, *"For I think that God has displayed us, the apostles, last, as men condemned to death;* (1 Corinthians 4:9). Our Greek word is here translated *has displayed.* Here it has the idea of shown or displayed in terms of appointed or caused to be. The idea of appointment usually has to do with a high office such as a king or overseer. But the Divine action is strangely varied with a different set of values. God has appointed or made Paul and the apostles as objects of death. They are participating in the very fate of Jesus in suffering and death. This is the reversal of rank found only in the Kingdom of God.

Paul describes a coming day when the *man of sin* or *the son of perdition* will exalt himself. There will come a time when he will exalt himself as God, *so that he sits as God in the temple of God, showing himself that he is God* (2 Thessalonians 2:3-4). Our Greek word here gives the idea of displayed or showing, but it has the undercurrent of proving. He is displayed as God so he is authenticated as God because of where he is sitting.

The final two times our word is used in the New Testament are in the Book of Acts. In the latter part of Acts, Paul is again in trouble with the Jews. He is brought before King Festus. The Jews *laid many serious complaints against Paul, which they could not prove* (Acts 25:7).

You can see the usage of the Greek word translated *prove*. There is no evidence to convict Paul of the charges. The idea of show or display is certainly present, but it goes beyond that concept. There is a purpose involved which is to authenticate or validate.

Now the fourth place for the use of this Greek word is found in our passage. *"Men of Israel, hear these words: Jesus of Nazareth, a Man attested by God to you,"* (Acts 2;22). We can plainly see that Jesus was displayed or shown before them. He is *the express image of His person* (Hebrews 1:3). *He is the image of the invisible God* (Colossians 1:15). But this showing was for a distinct purpose. There was a goal or end result in mind. God was *attesting*, authenticating, verifying, and proving *Jesus of Nazareth, a Man.* Consider the translation from the Amplified New Testament: *You men of Israel, listen to what I have to say: Jesus of Nazareth, a Man accredited and pointed out and shown forth and commended and attested to you by God* (Acts 2:22).

The impact of the statement is that God, the Father, is accrediting, pointing out, proving, authenticating, validating, showing forth, and commending something which evidently was very important to Him. Perhaps it was the great power of God. Through Jesus, God the Father attempts to prove to the world His great power. Or maybe it is love. Perhaps through Jesus God wants to prove that He really does love mankind. The list could go on and on. However, according to our passage God is only proving one single thing. It is *Jesus of Nazareth, a Man!* God is accrediting, pointing out, proving, authenticating, validating, showing forth, and commending *Jesus of Nazareth, a Man.*

The focus of God is upon Jesus. Everything He does through Jesus is to promote, lift up, and proclaim Jesus. He is proving Jesus! In order to grasp the full meaning of this, we will divide our study into two sections.

HE IS THE MESSIAH

In proving or attesting, *Jesus of Nazareth, a Man,* God the Father is authenticating who Jesus is. He is the Messiah. Do you realize how long the Father has been waiting to bring this one Man into this moment? In Genesis the record is given us of the sin of man. Adam and Eve violated the very desire and heart God had for them. But God would not let them go their own way. The dominant theme is that He promised redemption to them. He promised that the covenant relationship He had with them would be restored. This redemption would not come from an outside source, not even angelic beings. Even God could not set on His throne and manufacture this redemption. Man had gotten us into this mess and man would have to get us out. God promised that redemption would come from the victory the seed of woman would have over Satan. God assured Adam and Eve that redemption and restoration would be a reality in their lives and the history of their seed (Genesis 3:14-20). The Seed of the woman would restore, continue, and bring to full fruition God's Kingdom plans and goals. Jesus is this Seed!

Jesus is the *Man.* He is the One about whom the prophets have spoken. He is the One the universe has been groaning to embrace. Throughout the Old Testament, God kept the seed line open. God guarded and protected the coming of this One *Man*. He is the One God promised to sit on the throne of King David (Acts 2:30). He is the One God exalted to the right hand of the Father (Acts 2:33). He is the One God made Lord and Christ (Acts 2:36). The activity of God the Father is focused on this one *Man*. John the Baptist was made aware of this fact. He cried out, *"Behold! The Lamb of God who takes away the sin of the world! This is He of whom I said, 'After me comes a Man who is preferred before me, for He was before me,'"* (John 1:29-30).

In our passage, God the Father is approving, authenticating, and proving Jesus as this *Man*. He has done it through His life *by miracles, wonders and signs which God did through Him in your midst* (Acts 2:22). He has also done it through His death. This *Man* was *delivered by the determined purpose and foreknowledge of God* (Acts 2:23). This proof was also found in His resurrection. This *Man* is One *whom God raised up, having loosed the pains of death, because it was not possible that He should be held by it* (Acts 2:24).

Everything God has dreamed for mankind is found in this one *Man*. The phrase "in Christ" is used around two hundred times in the New Testament. This phrase is found eight times in Galatians, thirty-four times in Ephesians, and eighteen times in Colossians. A number of these references are not in the sense of incorporation but in the sense of instrumental. God has taken everything He wants us to have and placed it "in Christ." Christ is what He wants us to have! He *has blessed us with every spiritual blessing in the heavenly places in Christ* (Ephesians 1:3). The first chapter of the Book of Colossians is a list of those things found in the person of

Christ, this **Man.** In Him we have *redemption through His blood, the forgiveness of sins* (Colossians 1:14). *He is the image of the invisible God, the firstborn over all creation* (Colossians 1:15). He is the great Creator. In fact, *all things were created through Him and for Him* (Colossians 1:16). *He is before all things, and in Him all things consist* (Colossians 1:17). *And He is the head of the body, the church* (Colossians 1:18). The list goes on and on.

This is not about what Jesus has done or will do! This is about the Person of Christ! He is the One who is being proven, *attested*, accredited, pointed out, authenticated, validated, shown forth, and commended. God wants to convince us of Jesus. The message God gave the prophets in the Old Testament was Jesus. The message of the New Testament is Jesus. There are no activities of God or possibilities of touching God outside of Jesus. Jesus said, *"I am the way, the truth, and the life. No one comes to the Father except through Me,"* (John 14:6). Do you grasp the all inclusiveness of Jesus? He is everything! No wonder Paul cried, *For in Him dwells all the fullness of the Godhead bodily; and you are complete in Him, who is the head of all principality and power* (Colossians 2:9-10).

HE IS THE PROTOTYPE

God, the Father, is authenticating the actual Person of Christ. He is the fulfillment of the plans of God as revealed in the Old Testament. This is summarized in the term, Messiah. However, the key aspect of the position of Messiah is the concept of prototype. Peter definitely proclaims this in his message. It is an explanation of what has just happened to them on this Day of Pentecost. God has come to indwell them. The Holy Spirit has been poured out upon them. What does this mean exactly? Jesus is the explanation. Peter, throughout his message, consistently proclaims Jesus as *a Man*. But He is *a Man* through whom God is acting! This is plainly seen in His life (Acts 2:22), His death (Acts 2:23), and in His resurrection (Acts 2:24). Everything which happens in the life of Christ occurs because God the Father acts through Him. This is what a man filled with the Spirit of God looks like!

Adam was created to be this, but he yielded to self-centeredness. He became the source of his own living. God needed another man to restore and rebirth His dream. He decided not to create another man as He did Adam. God decided to become that *Man!* He emptied Himself of all He had as God and became *a Man*. He was *a Man* totally submitted and surrendered to the sourcing of God. Nothing would happen through Him but what God produced. He would be filled with the Holy Spirit, a product of God indwelling *a Man*.

Could such a dream be possible? It did not work the first time; would it work the second time? What would be different about the second Adam? The second Adam would need to correct, make up, pay for, and redeem all the first Adam produced by his sin. He would need to live in total response to the Spirit of God and thus produce an entirely new breed of people. He would be the prototype of a new kind of man. God desired to redeem all of mankind, but He must do it through *a Man*. Jesus is that *Man*. God proved in Christ that the fullness of the Holy Spirit works. Man can be filled with God and be what he ought to be. Peter proclaims to the crowd, "What just happened to us, the one hundred and twenty, is what was taking place in Christ. It can now happen in you!" God has proven it!

The great crowd was *cut to the heart* (Acts 2:37). They wanted to know what they should do in response to this truth. Peter immediately points them to Jesus. They are to repent which means to give up the former thought and embrace the second thought (Acts 2:38). Jesus is the second thought! They are to be baptized into Jesus (Acts 2:38). They are to seek Jesus! I am joining them in seeking Him now.

6

THE PROOF: HIS LIFE

ACTS 2:22

It is a new experience for the Jews of the Dispersion. They have just witnessed the outside God coming to live inside mankind in the lives of the one hundred and twenty disciples. Many manifestations of the occasion have raised a question in their minds. It is not a casual question. The question springs from the burning desire within them to experience the new thing God is doing. They are intense. They are seeking! Peter gives clear explanation under the strong inspiration of the Holy Spirit. This message will *cut* them *to the heart* (Acts 2:37).

The opening statement in Peter's message is focused on Jesus. He strongly emphasizes their present knowledge of Jesus, so he does not give them new information. After all, Christ lived His life in their midst. Peter clearly says that Jesus was *a Man.* He was born during their lifetime. He lived His life among them. They considered Him a man as they crucified Him. But Peter's statement to them is about *Jesus of Nazareth, a Man attested by God to you*

(Acts 2:22). Through the life of Christ (Acts 2:22), through His death (Acts 2:23), and through His resurrection (Acts 2:24) God was proving the Person of Jesus. God was not attempting to prove His great power; He had already accomplished this in creation (Romans 1:20). He was not declaring His great wisdom; for all He made is manifesting it (Psalms 104:24). He is accrediting, pointing out, proving, authenticating, validating, showing forth, and commending *Jesus of Nazareth, a Man.* This is His single focus!

This is such a key truth. God has placed all of His plans and purposes in the Person of Jesus. There is nothing or no one else! Jesus is the total focus of God. Everything God promotes is Jesus, and Jesus fulfills God's plan. There is no crisis where He will refer you to someone else. If you come to God with any question or issue, He is going to give you Jesus. It is very plain in the Scriptures that Christ is His eternal focus (Revelation 22:13).

What exactly is God's proof? The life of Christ is the beginning of the validation.

MIRACLES, WONDERS, AND SIGNS

Peter begins with the miracles, wonders and signs of Jesus. He opens His message with these words. *"Jesus of Nazareth, a Man attested by God to you by miracles, wonders, and signs which God did through Him in your midst, as you yourselves also know"* (Acts 2:22). This identical statement is made by the author of the Book of Hebrews. He spends an entire chapter presenting Jesus as superior to angels (Hebrews 1). He quotes scripture after scripture to validate it. He begins his second chapter with a severe warning. It is an appeal to focus on Jesus *lest we drift away* (Hebrews 2:1). In his warning he establishes a contrast. A word came from the angels which was so sure that everyone who disobeyed it was punished (Hebrews 2:2). If this was true for them, there is one possibility we shall escape. We have received greater revelation. The revelation which came to us was *first...spoken by the Lord* (Hebrews 2:3). It was then *confirmed to us by those who heard Him* (Hebrews 2:3). This fact is added above all of this, *God also bearing witness both with signs and wonders, with various miracles* (Hebrews 2:4).

The phrase, *wonders and signs,* is found some thirty times in the New Testament. These two words are normally used together. In the Book of Acts, the phrase, *wonders and signs*, appears four times, while *signs and wonders* is mentioned five times. These two words refer not to different classes of miracles, but to different aspects of the same miracle. The idea of *wonders* is the aspect of the miracle which is startling, imposing, or amazing. It is translated from the root Greek word which means "to keep, watch, connoting that which, due to its extraordinary character, is apt to be observed and kept in the memory." It is the overwhelming or shocking character of an event. The idea of *signs* is the spiritual end and purpose of the event. It is to lead to something out of and beyond itself. Thus a miracle is valuable not so much for what it is but for what it indicates of the grace and power of the Doer.

This is all verified by the word *miracles* in our text. This Greek word is where we get our word dynamite. It is used one hundred and nineteen times in the New

Testament. However, in the New King James Version it is only translated "miracles" seven times. In the Gospels it is most often translated "mighty works." The majority of times throughout the remaining New Testament it is translated "power." In our modern day understanding the translation of *miracles* in our passage is a bit misleading. No doubt Peter includes the great miracle feats of Christ, but he emphasizes the flow of the resource of God which accomplished these and other activities.

What Peter is saying becomes clear when you understand the heart content of each of these three words. There is a captivating amazement about the life of Christ (*wonders*). It is certainly seen in the deeds of His life which point to a spiritual end and purpose, the very Person of God (*signs*). Escaping through Christ is the very flow of the resource of God (*miracles*). Although His ministry activities and His deeds of special miracles are included, the life of Christ is the captivating amazement which points to a spiritual end and is the very flow of the Person of God. Everything about Jesus, His miracles, His relationships, His attitude, His mannerisms, and His every day living, all shock you and cause you to see the wonder of the Father.

This truth is further highlighted by the fact that all three of the words are in the dative case. There are several usages for the dative case. The most frequent corresponds to our use of the direct object. The direct object is what receives the action of the verb, but Peter has already given this to us in the Person of Jesus. *Jesus of Nazareth, a Man attested by God to you* is an accusative phrase which acts as the direct object. Now Peter gives us this additional phrase which begins with *miracles, wonders, and signs.* In our text the dative case of this phrase is an instrumental dative. It is used to indicate the means by which a verb's action takes place. It generally corresponds to the English prepositions "with" and "by." Thus in our text Peter's statement is translated *by miracles, wonders, and signs.* God authenticates, proves, attests, points out, and commends Jesus by the very flow of His resource through the life of Christ. This flow astounds and amazes the world and points to the spiritual end of the Father.

Another startling fact is that the Greek word translated *miracles* in our text is the same Greek word translated *power* in Jesus' description of the coming of the Holy Spirit within the believer. Jesus said, *"But you shall receive power when the Holy Spirit has come upon you: and you shall be witnesses to Me in Jerusalem, and in all Judea and Samaria, and to the end of the earth,"* (Acts 1:8). Whatever the Father was doing in Christ is now happening in the believer. Whatever the Father was doing in and through the believer was started in Christ. The Father proved this life in Christ as He authenticated, pointed out, attested, and commended this reality. Jesus Christ is God's proof of man's possibility.

The Greek word translated *miracles* (Acts 2:22) and *power* (Acts 1:8) is "dunamis." All Greek words which come from the same Greek root word "duna" have the meaning "of being able or capable." It even has the idea of "to will." There is a contrasting Greek word which will help us grasp the concept. It is "ischus." This Greek word stresses the fact of the ability while "dunamis" stresses the accomplishment. "Ischus" emphasizes the actual inherent power, while "dunamis" implies ability or capacity to perform.

If you picture "ischus" as having substance or being a thing, then you can picture the use of that substance of power to accomplish something (dunamis). Jesus promised we will have the use of this substance. It is not that we will possess the power as if it is ours. The activity, demonstration, and accomplishment of this power happens through us as it did in Christ. God, the Father, is the substance of the power and Jesus is the stage upon which it is performed. The life of Christ is the proof that sons of God can exist in the flesh. Peter cries out to those who are hungry. The life of God flowing and sourcing a man is proven in Christ and is now promised to you. You can experience it as well. He cries, *"For the promise is to you and to your children, and to all who are afar off, as many as the Lord our God will call"* (Acts 2:39).

GOD DID

Peter continues to highlight this proof through the life of Christ. *"Jesus of Nazareth, a Man attested by God to you by miracles, wonders, and signs which God did through Him in your midst, as you yourselves also know - "* (Acts 2:22). Notice the repetitive statement. The focus is on the activity and sourcing of God, the Father. Jesus is *a Man attested by God to you.* It happened through the instrument of *miracles, wonders, and signs which God did through Him.*

It intrigued me to discover the Greek word translated *did* is "poieo." We have highlighted this word repeatedly in previous studies. It is always used for the activities of Jesus. It accentuates not just the product of the deed, but the internal nature and sourcing of the deed itself. It is often used to speak of trees bearing fruit (Matthew 3:10). It is contrasted with duty, routine, and obligation which is something of an outside pressure and sourcing.

This same Greek word is used to describe God creating the heavens and the earth (Acts 4:24; 7:50; 14:15; 17:24). The physical creation came from the very internal nature of God. It is a reflection of the character and nature of who God is! No wonder Paul argues, *For since the creation of the world His invisible attributes are clearly seen, being understood by the things that are made, even His eternal power and Godhead,* (Romans 1:20).

Peter reveals that the attraction, amazement, and spiritual end of the sourcing which produced the life of Jesus is God, the Father. No wonder Jesus said to His disciples, *"If you had known Me, you would have known My Father also; and from now on you know Him and have seen Him,"* (John 14:7). Jesus is not the Father, but His life is the product of the Father's sourcing. Jesus went on to say, *"He who has seen Me has seen the Father,"* (John 14:9). No wonder Paul describes Jesus as *the image of the invisible God* (Colossians 1:15). The writer of the Book of Hebrews wrote that Jesus was the *brightness of His glory and the express image of His person* (Hebrews 1:3).

Peter cries out that the flowing resource which amazes us and points us to a spiritual end is God, the Father, demonstrating in and through Christ? This is his explanation of Pentecost. The one hundred and twenty believers experienced the very same thing in their lives. What they saw take place in Christ is now happening within them. As Jesus is sourced by the Father, so now the hundred and twenty disciples are being sourced by the Spirit of the Father. This is the beginning of the new level! Everything God has been doing up to this time is for this purpose. This same relationship is now promised to us (Acts 2:39).

THROUGH HIM

Peter is not done highlighting this truth. He restates it again. He proclaims, *"Men of Israel, hear these words: Jesus of Nazareth, a Man attested by God to you by miracles, wonders, and signs which God did through Him,"* (Acts 2:22). This Greek word translated *through* is very specific. It is a primary preposition which denotes the channel of an act. It is used for the instrument or intermediate cause. It highlights that which intervenes between the act of the will and the effect, and through which the effect comes. Thus it means "through, by, by means of."

Peter is very clear in what he proposes. Within the very nature of God, the Father, there is a creative power which is flowing through *a Man.* It produces an amazement and wonder in everyone who experiences this *Man.* The flow from the Father through this *Man* is for the purpose of proving, attesting, authenticating, pointing out, validating, and commending this *Man.* This *Man* is the channel or instrument through which God proves His supreme purpose for man. God wants to indwell man. Man was not built by God to source himself; but he was created for the sole purpose of being sourced by God. The realization of this has been lost for so long, it is questioned. Perhaps it is just a religious dream. Who will dare propose its possibility? Jesus is the answer. The reality of God living His life through mankind is proven in the Person of Jesus!

It started with Christ, but now has spread to the one hundred and twenty disciples. However, this is not intended for a few. The Jews of the Dispersion are included. It is to their children as well. But it is *to all who are afar off, as many as the Lord our God will call* (Acts 2:39). This is a promise!

IN YOUR MIDST

There is one more phrase which Peter adds to the life of Christ. *"Men of Israel, hear these words: Jesus of Nazareth, a Man attested by God to you by miracles, wonders, and signs which God did through Him in your midst, as you yourselves also know"* (Acts 2:22). Let me remind you of the subject and the verb of this long sentence. The Greek reflective pronoun translated *you yourselves* is the subject. The verb is the Greek word translated, *know.* Peter is only reminding them of what they have already grasped and understood. This is not a new revelation. As he closes this section of the life of Christ, he reminds them again of this reality. The life of Christ was lived *in your midst.*

The frequent use of this phrase in the Gospel of Luke and the Book of Acts cannot be overlooked. It underscores something remarkable and has strong theological implications. At the age of twelve, Jesus sits *in the midst* of the teachers in the temple (Luke 2:46). Jesus, the Master, assumes the role of a servant *in the midst* of His disciples (Acts 2:27). The disciples were terrified because Jesus Himself stood *in the midst* of them in His resurrected form (Luke 24:36). These are only examples of this emphasis.

This phrase is used immediately in the beginning of the Book of Acts. On the fortieth day of Christ's resurrection appearance, He is present among them (Acts 1:4). At the first recorded business meeting of the early church, Peter stood up *in the midst of the disciples* (Acts 1:15). This same emphasis is given in Peter *standing up with the eleven* as he preaches this great explanation to the Jews of the Dispersion (Acts 2:14).

Not surprisingly, Luke emphasizes this in Peter's sermon. The flowing resource of God, the Father, produces amazement and points to a spiritual end through *a Man* and was done *in the midst.* This was not accomplished in a vacuum. It is not ancient mythology. This is not drug induced. What God dreams of accomplishing in our lives is "a daily living kind of thing." There is no way to side step the truth. God has proven, attested, authenticated, pointed out, validated, and commended this *Man* called Jesus. God is seen in His life. He proved once and for all that God can actually indwell us and live His life through us. We can be filled with the very nature of God. The results can be awesome to our world. Our families can be amazed and experience again the very flow of the Person of God. This is a promise which is to us (Acts 2:39).

7

THE PROOF: HIS DEATH - A DIVINE PLAN

ACTS 2:23

How do you explain Pentecost? When you see someone filled with the Spirit of God, how do you explain what is happening within that person? The Spirit of Jesus has moved upon Peter to bring clarity to the Jews of the Dispersion and to us! This is not a matter of Peter's opinion. It is not about cultural environment. In reality, God gives us His explanation of this great event.

Pentecost must not be understood as simply an event. But this is true with all of the major events in the life of Christ. We see this forcibly in the cross. The crucifixion of Christ was not just a day in the life of Christ. The cross was not an experience for which Christ prepared and then from which He had to recuperate. This was the style of His life. He always lived the cross. It was fundamental in His thinking. It was His attitude and the expression of all his mannerisms. The cross style was the constant expression of the life of God living through Christ. That was Peter's explanation of Pentecost.

This same truth is found in the resurrection event. It was not just a great experience for Christ. The life of God flowing through a man could not be contained in death regardless of when or where it was confronted. The death of demonic possession could not survive the presence of the living God flowing through Christ (Matthew 8:29). *A Man* filled with the Spirit of God could go to the very heart of hell, but hell could not possess Him. He must be released *because it was not possible that He should be held by it* (Acts 2:24). The resurrection took place moment by moment in the life of Christ as He lived in a world filled with death.

This is true for the ascension or exaltation of Christ to the right hand of the Father. It was not just a great celebration to remember. The King who has been reigning from before time establishes a whole new Kingdom. In living through the fullness of the Spirit, Jesus actually opens a door to an entirely new breed, species of humanity. Pentecost is not simply an event for a moment. It is revelation of the heart of God. He establishes His Kingdom. It is not an event; it is a style!

How can we comprehend what is happening in one hundred and twenty men and women on this Pentecost Day? The explanation is based upon all that God had done in previous history. Peter begins with the text for his sermon as found in the prophecy of Joel. Pentecost is a product or fulfillment of the plan God has been working throughout the Old Testament. Everything has brought us to this point. Pentecost is the fulfillment of the dreams of God. He brings man back to the state in which He originally created Him. This is the restoration of mankind back to the full image of God.

The opening sentence of Peter's message is very simple. He says, *"Men of Israel, hear these words,"* (Acts 2:22). The second sentence, however, seems to be very complicated. It is a lengthy sentence which covers three verses. It appears the main verb is **know**, while the subject is **you yourselves.** Peter reminds them of what they already understand and have experienced. He forces them to verify the reality of what he proposes.

The focus of Peter's presentation is **Jesus of Nazareth.** But it is not **Jesus of Nazareth,** the Son of God (although this is true). He is **Jesus of Nazareth, a Man.** Certainly the audience being addressed understood this. They embraced Jesus as **a Man.** They crucified Him as **a Man.** They did not consider Him an angel or a ghost. However, there is one factor Peter desperately wants this crowd to understand. It is **Jesus of Nazareth, a Man attested by God to you.** The action of God was to prove Jesus. All the plans of God are fulfilled in Jesus. There is nothing outside of Christ. Jesus was not one of several plans; He was the plan. If you ask God for any solution to any problem, He is going to give you Jesus! He has no other answer.

How does this explain Pentecost? **Jesus of Nazareth, a Man** is God's explanation of Pentecost. Jesus was **a Man** filled with God. He was totally sourced by God. There was nothing happening in or through Jesus which was not the result of the Father. Jesus was the visible expression of the invisible Father. The sourcing of the Father through Jesus created amazement in His world which pointed everyone to the Father. All that is happening in Pentecost must be understood in the light of Christ. Peter explains Pentecost through Jesus' life (Acts 2:22), in Jesus' death (Acts 2:23), and by His resurrection (Acts 2:24). He begins with Pentecost being seen through the lens of the life of Christ. Jesus did not live as He lived because He was God (although He is most certainly God). Jesus' life was a product of what the Father did through Him. The amazing quality of Jesus' life (*wonders*) which pointed to the Father (*signs*) was the very flow of the Father through Christ (*miracles*). God has promised this same relationship to us (Acts 2:39).

Pentecost explained through the life of Christ is simple to understand. As God, the Father, moved through Jesus, *a Man*, He is now moving through us. Jesus was the prototype of what God intended for all of us. But His death presents something of a problem. Should not the power of God moving through Jesus deliver Him from such a cruel death as crucifixion? This particular death is one reserved for criminals, not individuals filled with God. The cross, in essence, is a sign of defeat. If the life of Christ is the wonder of God working through Him, His death is proof it does not win. Why did not the power of God contained within the life of Christ deliver Him from the cross? It would appear that God working and living through an individual would keep that person from the results of evil plans, sickness, and all things from the evil one. One can certainly understand the accusations at the foot of the cross. *"If you are the Son of God come down from the cross,"* they cried (Matthew 27:40). Others continued yelling, *"If He is the King of Israel, let Him now come down from the cross, and we will believe Him,"* (Matthew 27:42).

72

It is very important to consider that the writers of the Gospel accounts did not attempt to hide or belittle the cross. Matthew wrote His Gospel account as proof that Jesus was the Kingly Messiah. His main argument is one of authority. Over one half of his chapters are dedicated to the subject of the cross. He believed that the cross did not diminish the Divine authority, but increased it! How could this possibly be logical? Because it was planned! Jesus was not a victim; He was a victor!

Join me now in carefully investigating this study's verse (Acts 2:23).

HIM

The Greek word translated *Him* is in the accusative case, a direct object (Acts 2:23). This relates directly to *Jesus of Nazareth, a Man,* which is in the same case. It can be translated "this person" or "the same." There is no question to whom Peter refers. The ones Peter addresses definitely know Christ as *a Man*, and they know He was crucified by their hands. The dominant subject is *Him.* Everything in this verse points to *Him.*

BEING DELIVERED

The Greek word translated *being delivered* is also in the accusative case which makes it a part of this same direct object. However, this Greek word is not a verb. I realize that the way it is translated in our English text, it may appear as a verb. It is an adjective which gives content to *Him.* Therefore, this verse might read: "Him, the Delivered One."

The Greek word translated *being delivered* is only found in this passage in the New Testament. It is a compound word. It begins with the Greek word translated "from," and the Greek word meaning "given out or over, surrendered." This concept is given to us in abundance throughout the New Testament by the use of other words. Paul wrote, *"He who did not spare His own Son, but delivered Him up for us all, how shall He not with Him also freely give us all things?"* (Romans 8:32). The Greek word translated *delivered up* is an intensified form of "give." It designates the act whereby something or someone is transferred into the possession of another. This word is used one hundred and nineteen times in the New Testament.

BY THE DETERMINED PURPOSE AND FOREKNOWLEDGE OF GOD

What was the means of Christ's crucifixion? According to Peter it was *by the determined purpose and foreknowledge of God.* This statement is a dative clause, an instrumental dative. In the Greek language the word *by* is not there. It is used in the English translation because of the dative case. Peter explains the means of delivery. However, the article "the" is definitely present in the Greek writing and gives this phrase great strength.

The Greek word translated *determined* is a verb in the participle mood. In this case it acts as an adjective giving content to the *purpose and foreknowledge of God.* It occurs mostly in the writings of Luke. It is only found twice in the rest of the New Testament (Romans 1:4 and Hebrews 4:7). God is always the subject of this verb with only one exception (Acts 11:29). Luke consistently uses this word to refer to God's great plan of salvation. It comes from the word meaning "boundary, limit." It means to mark out definitely, determine, appoint, constitute. It is the *purpose and foreknowledge of God* which marked out or appointed the death of Christ on the cross.

The Greek word (boule) translated *purpose* is dominantly used in the writings of Luke. It appears only three other times (1 Corinthians, Ephesians, and Hebrews). This word is used for the will, purpose, or intention as the result of reflection. This is distinguished from another Greek word (thelema) as seen in the executing of that counsel. Is it possible to imagine the Trinity in council? The conclusion was the cross event.

The Greek word translated *foreknowledge* is an important and often misunderstood New Testament word. Most often we consider it simply knowing something before it happens. This would mean the great omniscience of God knew about the crucifixion of Christ before it happened. This gave God the opportunity to respond to this action with a counter action. However, the concept of this Greek word is beyond this simple "fore" knowledge. In this verse *foreknowledge* is in the instrumental dative case. This shows that it was the means by which Christ was delivered to His enemies. It is not that God simply knew of the crucifixion; He actually caused it. This verse is not about God seeing ahead of time what will take place; He is actively involved in bringing about His plan.

Let us examine *purpose* and *foreknowledge* together. God, through His omniscience, saw the crucifixion. In His sovereignty He had already designed a redemptive plan which focused on Christ. This plan came from the reflective counsel of the Trinity. He did not bend His plan to fit the activities of men; He encompassed the activities of men and bent them to fit His plan. This means the cross was the plan of God; it was the fulfillment of prophecy. This means God is actively responsible for the crucifixion of Christ.

How does this explain Pentecost? God, the Father, is proving Christ. Christ is the proof of the fullness of the God's Spirit. Here is how the Spirit-filled life appears. God proved Jesus by the amazing aspect of His daily living (*wonders*). He also proved Jesus by pointing us to a purpose beyond the activities He did (*signs*). It was caused by the consistent flow of His presence through this *Man* (*miracles*). But God also proved this same *Man* through His death. God flowed and lived His presence through the very essence of tragedy. Crucifixion was not in the best interest of Jesus' comfort. From the view of a world, things were not working out for Christ. It looked as if all of the events in the last week of His life have gone in reverse. Yet in the midst of the pain, suffering, and tragedy God was producing His supreme counsel through Christ.

If we are to understand the fullness of the Spirit of Christ in this setting, we must shift our focus. The Christian movement has focused on the comfort, happiness, and health of the individual. It is as if the outside God getting inside is for the purpose of fulfilling the individual. God lives within me to protect me, inspire me, fulfill me, and make me a wonderful person. All of these things may happen as a by-product of His presence. But the focus of the indwelling of God within the individual is the fulfillment of *the determined purpose and foreknowledge of God.* God has a plan which does not always focus on my immediate happiness and comfort. The fullness of the Spirit is not for the purpose of utilizing the power of God for my benefit; but for the dreams of God's eternal designs to be accomplished through my flesh. That may produce immediate discomfort, death, and denouncement.

Will I allow Christ to flow His life through me for the fulfillment of His dreams? Will I abandon my personal agenda for the accomplishment of His sovereign plan? Will I set aside my personal comfort to embrace the necessary suffering of His desires? Is this what Paul meant when he cried, *"that I may know Him and the power of His resurrection, and the fellowship of His sufferings, being conformed to His death,"* (Philippians 3:10)? Listen to his call, *"We are hard pressed on every side, yet not crushed; we are perplexed, but not in despair; persecuted, but not forsaken; struck down, but not destroyed - always carrying about in the body the dying of the Lord Jesus, that the life of Jesus also may be manifested in our body. For we who live are always delivered to death for Jesus' sake, that the life of Jesus also may be manifested in our mortal flesh,"* (2 Corinthians 4:8-11).

The fullness of the Spirit is not a seeking of pleasure, comfort, and happiness. It is a seeking of His life manifested in and through us as it was in Jesus. Would the life of Christ not be manifested in our flesh in much the same pattern as it was in His own flesh? Christ in you is not for the purpose of self-satisfaction. This is not about solving all my problems and making everything for my benefit. God has always had bigger plans than this. Will I allow Him to fulfill His dreams through me regardless of the cost? God proved Jesus as *a Man* through whom He could fulfill His dream in the world. Will I be such a man?

8

THE PROOF: HIS DEATH – MAN'S ACTION

ACTS 2:23

Academically understanding the crucifixion of Christ is no simple task. However, a spiritual understanding of this event drowns one in the depth of its reality. One can stay on the surface of the physical suffering or plunge into the heavenly realm where life is being changed. It is here we intend to journey. I am not sure how capable I personally am to make this journey; therefore, we must depend as always on Christ who has already walked this path.

Under the inspiration of the Holy Spirit, Peter is leading us. His message (Acts 2:17-39) must be understood as an explanation of the Pentecost event. One hundred and twenty men and women have just experienced the outpouring of the Spirit of Christ. The Jews of the Dispersion, numbering over three thousand, have been witnesses. In their amazement, they ask, **"Whatever could this mean?"** (Acts 2:13). Here in the context of this perplexity and questioning, Peter gives us insight into the heart of Pentecost.

The second sentence of his sermon is long and complex (Acts 2:22-24). The heart of the matter focuses on *Jesus of Nazareth, a Man attested by God to you* (Acts 2:22). The Greek word translated *attested* means "to display, show, validate, commend, and authenticate." What has just taken place in the lives of the believers has already been displayed, validated, or authenticated. This was done by God in the Man called Christ. He is the explanation of Pentecost. What took place in Him is now happening in the believers.

Peter continues in this great sentence to explain how God has proceeded with this proof. It took place in the life of Jesus (Acts 2:22). Jesus' life was a direct result of the flowing resource of the Spirit of God (*miracles*). The sourcing of the Spirit produced an amazement among all who came in contact with the life of Christ (*wonders*), and it always points them back to the Father from whence it came (*signs*). This is Peter's explanation of Pentecost. The believers are experiencing this same flow of the Spirit of God through their lives as Jesus did through His.

It is somewhat more difficult to embrace Peter's next thought (Acts 2:23). As the sourcing of the Holy Spirit produced the life of Christ, He also produces the death of Christ which is equally a demonstration of the resource of God. The activities of Jesus' life validated the reality of Pentecost; His death equally authenticated this filling of the Holy Spirit.

Immediately, this gives us the proper view of the crucifixion of Christ. Jesus was not a victim; He was a victor. As His miraculous life was a fulfillment of the sourcing and plans of God, so His death is the plan of God. God did not see in the future what wicked men were going to do and quickly adjust His plan to accommodate the actions of men. The Trinity actually counseled together and devised the crucifixion plan (*determined purpose*). God did not perceive what man was going to do and adjust His plans to include it; He planned His actions and included man in those plans (*purpose and foreknowledge of God*).

PURPOSE

There are several major conclusions to be understood from this truth. The first is the purpose of Pentecost. The indwelling of the Spirit of Christ is not for the benefit, aid, pleasure, or comfort of man. God did not create man only to discover he had major flaws. Upon discovering these weaknesses and inabilities God corrected them with the addition of Pentecost. Man was made in the image of God, which of necessity demanded the very indwelling of God's nature and life within man. The original purpose of man was all we see happening in the life and death of Jesus. The focus was never the comfort and pleasure of man's personal life, but the fulfillment of the dream of God. Mankind was to be the display of the very heart and nature of God. Jesus displayed the Father through His life. The visible image of the invisible God was revealed in Christ (Colossians 1:15). Jesus could truthfully say to His disciples, *"He who has seen Me has seen the Father,"* (John 14:9).

This is our destiny. We have the staggering privilege of being the body of God in our day. The issue is not our personal comfort and desires, but the fulfillment of God's dreams and plans. The eternal plan of God contained within the mind of God has come to indwell us. God did not create us and then come up with a plan. God first had a plan and we were created out of that dream. Our destiny is to fulfill the dream of God. Our life is completed in that fulfillment.

An example of this is John the Baptist. He was filled with the Holy Spirit from his birth (Luke 1:15). He was not shaped by his culture; his life was not dictated by traditions. His goal was never comfort or ease. Even in the early, tragic end of a successful ministry, he was being used by this indwelt Spirit. He was the forerunner; he was created by God for this purpose. Of necessity this involved the cross style. There was a call on His life beyond his personal desires. He was filled with God.

God has an eternal plan. If Pentecost is experienced in our lives it will mean the fulfillment of that plan even to the expense of our personal pleasure. We must remember this is not "an add on" for an exclusive few. This is the basic style of Christianity. This is not "an advanced level" for those who are especially skilled. This is the normal. This is the fulfillment of the destiny of man!

PROVIDENCE

What Peter is proposing in this one great sentence (Acts 2:22-24) is based upon the Scripture taken from the Book of Psalms (16:8-11). He is constantly saturating his message with the Scriptures. As we read this passage (Acts 2:25-28), the tone of this Scriptural basis becomes very clear. It is one of extreme confidence in the goodness of God. Listen to his words. *I foresaw the Lord always before my face* (Acts 2:25). The idea of *foresaw* is literally "to see before us," that is, "as present with us, to regard as being near." It conveys the idea of putting your confidence in someone, relying on him, or expecting assistance from him. The phrase *always before my face* expresses the Lord is always present to help me and to deliver me out of all my troubles.

This confidence produces great rejoicing and gladness (Acts 2:26). This was certainly expressed in the life of Christ. The author of the Book of Hebrews instructs us, *"looking unto Jesus, the author and finisher of our faith, who for the joy that was set before Him endured the cross, despising the shame, and has sat down at the right hand of the throne of God,"* (Hebrews 12:2). The wonder of the Spirit-filled life is the ability to look beyond the immediate circumstances to the fulfillment of the will of God, which is always good. The absolute certainty of this goodness is solidly located in the character and heart of God. It has to be good because He is good. This is His dream; it has rushed forth from the very heart of His inner drive. This dream is totally motivated by love, which is His character. Any discomfort for the moment is only for the fulfillment of the great plan of His love. You and I get to be included in this great plan which is really who He is. No wonder there is joy. He is directing and sourcing our living and our dying.

This confidence in the goodness and love of God produces singing in the midnight hours when one is in jail with a beaten back (Acts 16:25). When one is gripped with the fulfillment of the dreams of God, there is joy in the suffering of the cross. Pentecost is the flow of the

Spirit of Christ through the life of the believer (*miracles*). It produces amazement (*wonders*) and always points back to Christ (*signs*). However, this same flow of the Spirit may lead us into discomfort and pain. Both can be produced by the flowing life of God through the believer.

PROTECTION

There is one other important factor concerning the sourcing of God that brings us to death. There is great safety here! This is a vital part of the explanation of *taken by lawless hands, have crucified, and put to death,"* (Acts 2:23). There is absolutely no attempt on the part of Peter to eliminate the responsibility and guilt of those he addresses. Indeed, the crucifixion of Christ was because of *the determined purpose and foreknowledge of God.* It is by the hand of a sovereign God that Jesus was crucified. However, this does not dismiss the willing participation of evil men. They crucified Christ by an act of their free will. With their lips they quoted the law, but with their hands they willingly broke the law. Time after time the Spirit flowed through Jesus to call them to embrace God's Messiah. Time and again they rejected. There is no reduction of guilt (Acts 2:37).

It is amazing to realize that God used *the lawless hands* of men to accomplish His Divine purpose, yet never violated their will. The total sovereignty of God is presented alongside the complete responsibility of man. This great paradox is presented repeatedly throughout the Scriptures. It is boldly illustrated in the betrayal of Christ by Judas. Jesus said this about Judas. *"And truly the Son of Man goes as it has been determined, but woe to that man by whom He is betrayed!"* (Luke 22:22). Men are responsible not for God's plans but for their own sins.

The order of the Greek words as given in our text becomes very important at this point. Notice the phrase *have taken* is not present in the Greek text. It has been added in order to aid the flow of the English translation. Luke begins the verse with the Greek pronoun translated *Him*. He definitely wants you to understand he is still referring to *Jesus of Nazareth, a Man.* This is immediately followed by the Greek phrase translated *by the determined purpose and foreknowledge of God.* It is then that the Greek adjective, *being delivered*, appears. Remember this adjective modifies the opening pronoun of the verse which refers to Christ as the Delivered One. Immediately following this is the Greek phrase translated *by lawless hands.* This is the second instrumental dative phrase which expresses the means by which the action of this verse takes place. The next Greek word is translated *have crucified.* This is a Greek verb in the participle form. It is acting as an adjective. However, it is in the nominative case which means it modifies the main subject of the sentence. Peter is literally calling this great crowd the crucifiers. Finally the last Greek word in the text is translated *put to death.* It is a verb in the indicative mood which means it is a simple statement of fact. This Greek word means simply to kill or murder.

So the structure of this verse is as follows: *Him* (Christ), the *delivered* One, was *put to death by the determined purpose and foreknowledge of God* and by *lawless hands* of you who *crucified.* One easily sees that the action of this part of Peter's long sentence is the Greek word translated *put to death.* Then Peter lists two equally instrumental datives which tell the means by which this was done. One is *by the determined purpose and foreknowledge of God;* the second is *by lawless hands.* If our lives are affected or influenced *by lawless hands* of men, are we not constantly experiencing in our lives evil things over which no one has control? The dreams and plans of God are constantly being thwarted because of the interference of wickedness. No one would deny there is a sense in which this is true. Theology teaches us the will of God abides in two categories. There is the primary will of God which was and is His supreme desire. However, there is also the secondary will of God which He accepts. It is the primary will of God that everyone should be saved. However, there is the will of God which accepts the free will of man. This presents the certainty that not all will accept His primary will.

How does this explain Pentecost? Pentecost is about the *determined purpose and foreknowledge* of God being accomplished through *a Man.* It is not about the personal pleasure or comfort of that individual. God's dream and design must be accomplished through man. We have the privilege of linking with and being used by a sovereign God to fulfill the destiny of His creative desire. Nothing can stop this! In the fullness of the Spirit our lives are not determined by the whim of mystical fate. We are not at the mercy of the forces of evil. While our fellow man has free will and is responsible for his response, he will not be allowed to determine or affect the fulfillment of the dreams of God through our lives! The Spirit-filled believer is safe in the dreams of God regardless of how things appear in his circumstances. No wonder the author of the Book of Hebrews calls this "rest,"

(Hebrews 4). Now we understand why Paul and Silas sang at midnight in the midst of the pain of their beaten backs (Acts 16:25). We can now view the heroes of faith in a new way (Hebrews 11). Those looking forward to and those who actually received were all given vision through the eyes of the Spirit. Nothing could stop them! They were used by God to conquer their world. They became the instruments for the fulfillment of the dreams of God.

The staggering reality is that this is not true for the individual outside of Pentecost. If the outside God has not come inside, there is no safety. When I am in charge of my own life and destiny, there is no control. I am not capable of warding off the forces of evil and the *lawless hands* of men. My best intentions and attempts will not be enough to protect. There is no purpose found in the crucifixions of my life. I am being moved from situation to situation by the mystical hand of fate with no reason or destiny. Does this not cause us to go to our knees for our children? There is only one safe place for my family. My children and my spouse must know the fullness of the Spirit.

God has proven this in Christ. What we see in Jesus' life and in His death is now ours. He is the beginning of the new relationship with God. Man can be filled with God. The outside God has come to be inside. We can be like Jesus!

9

THE PROOF: HIS RESURRECTION

ACTS 2:24

The staggering truth of Peter's explanation of Pentecost is before us (Acts 2:22-39). Verses twenty-two through twenty-four are one long sentence. Verse twenty-four is a clause which presents the conclusion. Peter addresses the Jews of the Dispersion, the number of which is several thousand. The main subject is *you yourselves* (Acts 2:22). The main verb is *know* (Acts 2:22). He simply relates to them what they already *know.* They have the knowledge and understanding of *Jesus of Nazareth, a Man attested by God to you* (Acts 2:22). The focus of the statement is on the reality of God proving, attesting, validating, and authenticating the person of Christ. Peter then begins to list three distinct ways in which God has proven Jesus. We must interpret these facts in light of Pentecost. Peter gives an explanation of what has just happened (Acts 1:1-4).

As he begins, Peter highlights the life of Christ (Acts 2:22). Jesus, *a Man,* is the channel through which God manifested Himself. God revealed His person

9

through Christ (*miracles*) which amazed and astonished His world (*wonders*). This revelation always points back to the Father (*signs*). However, this same life of God brings Jesus to death (Acts 2:23). Intimacy with God is not about our comfort, ease, and convenience. Intimacy is about the dreams and plans of God. Many times this brings us to a cross. Be assured God will never leave us there. Our passage is Peter's emphasis on the resurrection (Acts 2:24). The purpose of all of this is to explain Pentecost. God wants to accomplish this same thing in each personal life. It is a promise!

The subject of the clause in our text is **God.** He is the Prime Mover in the process, through the life of Christ. The main verb is **raised up.** This Greek word is the most common verb used for the resurrection of Christ. It is also used in its noun form (Acts 2:31), but Peter stresses the verb form of this word in his message (Acts 2:24-32). The Greek word used in our text is an action word, a verb. It is the same Greek word used for what happened to Peter as the Spirit of God moved upon him to preach at Pentecost (Acts 2:14). The focus of the resurrection of Christ is not on the event but on the action of God within the event. Our culture focuses on the event; the New Testament focused on the moving of God which is the heart of the event. We claim our salvation as an event; however, the heart of our salvation is the movement of God which was present then and now! Our salvation is not a noun; it is a verb.

Another surprising detail about this Greek word for **raised up** is its tense. Each time this word is used as a verb in connection with the resurrection of Christ, it is in the aorist tense. The only exception is when Jesus is quoted as speaking about His coming death and resurrection (Mark 9:31; 10:34). In these passages, the future tense is used. The New Testament writers apparently viewed the resurrection as only in the aorist tense. There is nothing like this tense in the English language. In its beginning stages, the Greek language only had the aorist tense. It was the "non-tense." Past, present, and future were developed later. The view of the aorist tense is external. It takes one outside the event or action, and it is seen from the beginning and the end. There is no concern with when it will happen; it is as if it has always been. Past, present and future are internal views. One stands in the middle of the event and views it as it happens (present), or as it is going to take place (future), or as it has already occurred (past). The aorist is the nearest tense we have to describe the view of God. He is outside the time zone and He views the resurrection as eternal.

In our passage Peter is not just reminding his listeners of an event which took place in the past, but he focuses them on the movement of God in Christ. It was not just in the past, nor is it in the future. It is not just in the now, which is the present tense. What God is doing in Christ has an eternal flavor to it. The time restraints do not apply. Peter develops this idea as his message progresses. This must be the reason John, in his Gospel account, consistently refers to the believer as already having eternal life. Within the framework of our time zone, the believer lives in the aorist tense.

One other factor concerning the verb of our passage is the active voice. This means the subject is responsible for the action of the verb. There is no question God is the source of all that is happening in Christ. Peter says so several times, leaving no room for argument or adjustment (Acts 2:24, 32). This is true in Jesus' exaltation as well as in the receiving of the promise of the Father (Acts 2:33). It even applies to His Lordship (Acts 2:36).

The next statement in our passage is *having loosed the pains of death.* The verb *having loosed* is in the participle form which makes it an adverb in this passage. It means to "untie, release, or untangle." It gives content to the verb translated *raised up.* This is a word which corresponds to the Greek word translated *should be held.* Peter paints the same picture twice for emphasis. This relates to the *pains of death.* The Greek word translated *pains* is in the feminine gender. It seems to relate to the idea of the birth pains of child bearing. Death could not keep Jesus any more than a pregnant woman can keep a child in her womb.

Then Peter explodes into the rest of the statement to explain *because* or why! He adds this last clause to his large sentence. God proved Jesus in His life (Acts 2:22) and in His death (Acts 2:23). He now gives us information to deepen our understanding in relation to the reaction of death to the life of the Spirit within *a Man.* He takes us beyond an activity God does for Jesus in raising Him from the dead. He explains Pentecost to the Jews of the Dispersion. He reveals to us how death responds when an individual filled with the Holy Spirit enters its realm.

He begins with *it was.* It is a translation from the Greek word "een." This Greek word means "to be" and is a focus on existence. This Greek word is contrasted with the Greek word "ginomai" which means "to become." These two Greek words are contrasted in John's Gospel account in the first chapter. Jesus is the "een" One (John 1:1). John the Baptist is the "ginomai" one (John 1:16). "Een" has an eternal value to it. This same Greek word (een) is used for the name of God at the burning bush. It is used in the great "I AM's" of Jesus. In addition to this, it is in the imperfect tense which means something happens in the past and continues into the present." God proved this man called Jesus. God moved His life through Jesus as He lived; He produced His death. But God continued to source Him even into the realm of death.

In this great sentence, Peter's concluding statement is *because it was not possible that He should be held by it* (Acts 2:24). A slight change was made in the translation which makes a tremendous difference in the interpretation of the statement. The justification for the change has to do with the Greek word which is translated *possible.* It is the Greek word "dunamis." We contrasted this word with the Greek word "ischus" in a previous study. "Ischus" is ability or resource. "Dunamis" is the flow of that resource in action. "Dunamis" is the Greek word translated *miracles* (Acts 2:22) and *power* (Acts 1:8). In light of this, the negative *not* should be connected to the Greek word translated *should be held.* The verse might read; *it was* (een, the state of being) *because* (why) *possible* (the flowing life of God) *should not be held by it.*

The "een" of the life of God was so powerful within this Man that it was *not possible* for Jesus to remain captured. This Greek word "dunamis" is an adjective translated "possible" which gives content to *it was.* Whatever is contained within *death* does not have the power or ability to contain the life of God sourcing *a Man.* Death exerts all the power it has and still cannot contain *a Man* filled with God.

The Greek word translated *should be held* is a verb in the infinitive mood. In the English grammar it is usually introduced with the word "to." This verb does not stand on its own but requires the main verb, *was* or "een." The negative ability to hold Jesus in death is tied into the existence of the life of God contained within *a Man.* This Greek word actually means "to forcibly seize, take hold of, arrest, or take into custody." It is absolutely impossible for death, in exerting this authority or power, to hold Jesus! It is because of the "een" (eternal) of God.

It is very significant that this verb is in the present tense. In the Greek language this means "now with a continual action." The present tense is moving from moment to moment and remains present. The resource of the nature of God, which is flowing through Jesus, is continually defeating the grasping ability of death. It is in the passive voice which means the subject is receiving the action. Since a verb in the infinitive tense does not stand alone, but relies on the main verb, its subject is also the subject of the main verb. The subject of the main verb in our clause is *it,* referring to the state of being, which is the flowing life of God. It was not death's fault that it could not hold Jesus. Death was acted upon by something greater than itself. Death could never hold the living nature of God. Peter is not saying that death could at one time hold the nature of God, but has lost its ability. Nor is he saying that Jesus earned the right to be liberated from the grip of death. His statement is that death has never had the ability to contain a man filled with the Spirit of God.

Peter attempts to explain Pentecost to the Jews of the Dispersion. The Spirit of God has filled one hundred and twenty believers. What does this mean for these Jews of the Dispersion? It means to them exactly what it meant to Jesus. Death could not hold Him; death cannot hold them. He is not saying that they are liberated from the grasp of death because Jesus paid the penalty; rather He is saying they are liberated from the holding power of death because of the fullness of the nature of God indwelling them. It is the indwelling nature of God which makes man free from the binding power of death. If we are sourced by God we will not die; if we are sourced by death we are bound already and are dead.

To help clarify this, I would like for you to journey with me through the Gospel according to John. "Eternal life" becomes a common phrase in this writing. He starts with a strong emphasis on life. He gives us a proper picture of Jesus both from the eternal view as well as the human view. *In Him was life, and the life was the light of men,* (John 1:4). Again we must consider the Greek word "een" which is translated *was*. It has an eternal flavor to it, the state of existence, or to be. If we are not in relationship with Him who is life, we have no life in us. John highlights this truth from the outset of his Gospel account. Now let's go to the close of his account (John 20:31). *But these are written that you may believe that Jesus is the Christ, the Son of God, and that believing you may have life in His name.* Here he has captured his entire purpose for writing this account. In doing so he relates the necessity of having an intimate relationship with Christ (*believing*) which gives life. Is there any doubt that the theme of his writing is "life found in Christ?"

In between these two statements numerous references to life will be highlighted. All of these references will come from the lips of Christ as He speaks. There is one exception when Peter confesses directly to Jesus, *"Lord, to whom shall we go? You have the words of eternal life,"* (John 6:68). It is in the early chapters **Nicodemus, a ruler of the Jews** appears. Within this discussion we discover our own limited knowledge as Nicodemus views life from a physical perspective. The very imagery of **born again** bespeaks ushering us into a new level of living greater than the present physical. The epitome of Jesus' message is given in a verse you have memorized. He says, *"For God so loved the world that He gave His only begotten Son, that whoever believes in Him should not perish but have everlasting life,"* (John 3:16). The Greek word translated *have* is in the present tense. This implies continual possession. The Greek word translated *everlasting* is also translated *eternal* in the previous verse. He says, *"That whoever believes in Him should not perish but have eternal life."* The Greek grammar and the Greek words of the last phrase in both statements is the same. The Greek word translated *eternal* has the idea of perpetual. When it is applied to life, it means the life which is God's and hence is not affected by the limitations of time. All of this is directly connected to the life of the Spirit within the believer (John 3:8). Jesus also connects this same life with the judgment in this passage. He says, *"He who believes in Him is not condemned; but he who does not believe is condemned already, because he has not believed in the name of the only begotten Son of God,"* (John 3:18).

It did not take long for the pressure to increase to the point the Jews wanted to kill Jesus. In the midst of these feelings, Jesus said, *"Most assuredly, I say to you, he who hears My words and believes in Him who sent Me has everlasting life, and shall not come into the judgment, but has passed from death into life,"* (John 5:24). What an encouraging statement! Jesus uses the same present tense grammar here. It is a bold statement to proclaim that anyone who is filled with the Spirit of Christ has eternal life now and will have eternal life continually. The Spirit of Christ contained within an individual cannot be held by death and death cannot inflict the judgment.

In the context of the feeding of the five thousand, Jesus addresses the issue of bread. Since the Jews were complaining about Him, Jesus saw it necessary to give additional information. He said, *"I am the living bread which came down from heaven. If anyone eats of this bread, he will live forever; and the bread that I shall give is My flesh, which I shall give for the life of the world,"* (John 6:51). Now the Jews quarreled among themselves about how this could possibly be. Jesus went on to say, *"Whoever eats My flesh and drinks My blood has eternal life, and I will raise him up at the last day,"* (John 6:54).

The Jews became so frustrated they fell into name calling. They said to Jesus, *"You are a Samaritan and have a demon* (John 8:48). He denied that He possessed a demon but identified with the Father who indwelt Him. He could not simply think about Himself, but hurriedly said, *"Most assuredly, I say to you, if anyone keeps My word he shall never see death,"* (John 8:51). They could not comprehend His words and immediately took up rocks to stone Him (John 8:59).

As Jesus attempts to illustrate the truth, He speaks of being the Good Shepherd. He applies the various aspects of a shepherd's life to His own. He says, *"The thief does not come except to steal, and to kill, and to destroy. I have come that they may have life, and that they may have it more abundantly,"* (John 10:10). In the context of all Jesus says about life, this abundant life must certainly have at its heart eternal life produced by His presence within the sheep. He goes on to proclaim, *"And I give them eternal life, and they shall never perish; neither shall anyone snatch them out of My hand,"* (John 10:28).

Lazarus' death gave rise to a great teaching opportunity about eternal life. All the feelings and emotions we are prone to experience in the midst of death were present with Mary and Martha. With a tone of accusation, Martha told Jesus that Lazarus would not have died if He had been there. Jesus assured her that Lazarus would rise again, but Martha interpreted it to mean in the future resurrection. It was then that Jesus said, *"I am the resurrection and the life. He who believes in Me, though he may die, he shall live. And whoever lives and believes in Me shall never die. Do you believe this?"* (John 11:25-26). Is this reality? The resurrection has already taken place in those who believe in Jesus.

There are three major chapters in the Gospel according to John which are focused exclusively on the coming Pentecost event (John 14, 15 and 16). Verse after verse is dedicated to the coming of the Holy Spirit. These powerful words are spoken to the disciples in a private setting in the upper room before the Garden of Gethsemane event and His crucifixion. He tries to get them focused on what He is going to experience and where it will take them. They are going to know intimacy with God. He said, *"At that day you will know that I am in My Father, and you in Me, and I in you,"* (John 14:20). How could there be a tighter or more intimate relationship than that? He even told the parable of The True Vine (John 15:1-8) to illustrate this oneness. Just before going to the Garden of Gethsemane, He broke into His great high priestly prayer (John 17). In the third verse of that prayer He cried, *"And this is eternal life, that they may know You, the only true God, and Jesus Christ whom You have sent,"* (John 17:3). In previous studies we have discovered the Greek word for *know* is "ginosko." It is not simply about knowledge or information. It is a relational term. It is the Biblical word for the most intimate relationship in the marriage union (Matthew 1:25). Intimacy and relationship with God is eternal life.

Now we view this great Gospel truth through the eyes of Pentecost. Intimacy, knowing, believing have all come together in the fullness of the Holy Spirit. God has come to indwell man. God, who is life, cannot be contained in death. The flowing resource of God living through Jesus may have brought Him to death, but death could not hold Him. It was child's play; there was no contest. The flowing resource of death does not match the flowing resource of Life! This is promised to us!

Think of the staggering ramifications of this for your life. We live in a world where death is constantly confronting and surrounding us. Spiritual death constantly attempts to swallow the church. Where are the people of life? Who will be filled with the Spirit and march into their world?

10

THE PROOF: DEATH IS CONQUERED

ACTS 2:24

What is Peter saying about the resurrection of Christ in relation of Pentecost? That is what we desire to discover. In our last study we attempted a detailed analysis of verse twenty-four. Everything in Peter's message must be interpreted in light of what has just happened to one hundred and twenty believers. The Jews of the Dispersion witnessed the event and they wanted to know, *"Whatever could this mean?"* (Acts 2:13).

Peter's explanation focuses on *Jesus of Nazareth, a Man attested by God to you* (Acts 2:22). God proved, authenticated, and validated the fullness of the Spirit in Christ. What the life of God in Christ did for Him, it will do for all men! It is now happening in the one hundred and twenty believers and is promised to us. One of the startling factors is the issue of death and resurrection (Acts 2:23-24). The fullness of Christ in the believer is not just for the sake of this present living experience. Christ is to live His life through the believer, not just on concrete streets, but on streets of gold as well. The indwelling of the Spirit is an eternal experience. It defines our essence as Christians. To remove this is to cease to be Christian either here on earth or in heaven.

The life of God flowing through Jesus not only produced His living, but also produced His death (Acts 2:23). It has become important to me for the Spirit of God to produce my death. It is then it will have significance. The death of Christ counted in the redemptive plan of God. Should not my death count in the same plan? John the Baptist's death played a key role in preparing for the death of Christ. Could not my death be used in such a manner? Am I at the whim of accidents or freak events? Does happen-chance dictate my existence? Should I not be filled with God as Jesus was and in this oneness find direction even for my death?

This also applies to the resurrection from the dead. Everything Peter explains about the experience of Christ becomes mine when the same Spirit flows through me. The flowing life of God in Jesus produced His life, death and resurrection. The picture is vivid concerning the **resurrection** (Acts 2:24). Jesus did not enter into death and hell only to be trapped there. God, the Father, did not need to rush to His rescue and raise Him from the dead. Rather the picture painted is that of a man filled with the Spirit of God. When the flowing life of God in a man confronts death and hell, hell and death are powerless.

Obviously, the significance of the resurrection is seen in light of the greatness of death. Death is a strong enemy. We know that it takes the great movement of God to bring victory from it. In our passage, death is referenced three times. Verse twenty-three concludes with it: *Him, being delivered by the determined purpose and foreknowledge of God, you have taken by lawless hands, have crucified, and put to death.* It appears twice in our present text: *whom God raised up, having loosed the pains of death, because it was not possible that He should be held by it* (Acts 2:24).

Peter uses three completely different words to make this reference. The Greek word translated *put to death* (Acts 2:23) is "anaireoe." It is from two words: an emphatic or up (ana) and to take (haireoe). This is translated "to slay, murder, or take off." This corresponds with the idea of death as that which imprisons an individual or holds them. This Greek word is used as a verb in the clause of our long sentence. The emphasis is on the movement or the action of death. The Greek word in our text (Acts 2:24) translated *death* is "thanatos" which is a noun. Then at the end of the verse, death is referred to by a pronoun. However, in each case they are related to the illustrated action which is happening. In the first case, it is the entangling pains likened unto child birth, which is being untied or *loosed.* The pronoun which refers to death relates to "take hold of" or "forcibly seize."

Peter highlights the greatness of the resurrection by placing it firmly in the context of the severity of death. He points out the strangle hold of death upon a man so strongly, the resurrection is almost lost in the tragedy. This again reminds us, we must know the strength of our enemy in order to understand the greatness of our Conqueror. For this reason, let me remind you of the exposition of this verse (our previous study on Acts 2:24).

In this long sentence, **God** is definitely the subject of this climatic clause. The resurrection is presented to us in the verb form (**raised up**). This emphasizes the fact that it is not an event but a movement of God within the event. This resurrection verb is in the aorist tense. This places us outside the event which gives us an eternal view of what God is doing. It is not about what God is doing, has done, or will do, but simply about what happens when a man filled with the Spirit comes in contact with death. Death can no more hold that man than a pregnant woman can keep her child in her womb. Death in all of its fury cannot contain the life of God filling a man!

CAUSE OF DEATH

In light of this expositional study, it might be wise for us to understand the Biblical background concerning death. Let's begin with a deep awareness that death is simply the opposite of life and was never intended. As seen in our study (Acts 2:22-24), death is all that is experienced outside of the fullness of the Spirit of Christ. It was intended by God that man should live sourced by God. The moment man is not sourced by God, he is dead. This reveals to us the reality of life and death. Life is Christ; death is the absence of Christ. Anything outside of Christ is death. No wonder John cries, *"In Him was life, and the life was the light of men,"* (John 1:4). This places life completely beyond the simple definition of breathing, eating, or functioning. Death is not the absence of these things. This leads us to the conclusion that death is not a natural process. It may be the way man is now, but it was not the way man was created by God. Man was created by

God to be sourced by God, thus to live. Death is foreign, something to be greatly feared. It is no more regarded as a natural process than the resurrection. It is caused!

What is the cause of death or separation from the sourcing of God? It is contained within the very pride and self-will of man. Consistently this cause is called "sin!" Therefore, when one seeks to discover the cause of death he is really seeking the cause of sin. Death shapes our concept of sin. Paul said, *"For the wages of sin is death, but the gift of God is eternal life in Christ Jesus our Lord,"* (Romans 6:23). If life is found only "in" Christ, then death is found "outside of Christ." Our text (Acts 2:22-24) teaches us that a man sourced by the Spirit of Christ is alive, but when he is sourced out of himself he is dead. Therefore, death is caused by self-sourcing. This must become the definition for all sin – self-sourcing. Sin has always been man wanting to live out of himself and not living out of Christ. It is a sourcing issue. To identify sin by deeds is to miss the heart of the matter. Sin is never about right and wrong. Even the best deed sourced by man remains a sin and produces death.

Perhaps this helps us understand the fallacy of the law. Understanding this principle, it is easy to see the law never brings life, but always produces death. Even if man keeps the entire law, he lives in death. For some reason, chapter seven in the Book of Romans has become controversial. Paul simply presents mankind from the viewpoint of the law. He strongly declares that sin is produced by the law (Romans 7:7-12). He says, *"And the commandment, which was to bring life, I found to bring death,"* (Romans 7:10). He further says, *"The law is holy, and the commandment holy and just and good,"* (Romans 7:12). So the problem is not the law. The problem is man relying on himself to keep the law. Paul calls this "sin!"

He then breaks into a powerful discourse of the struggle contained within the heart of man (Romans 7:13-25). Listen to his plea. *"Has then what is good become death to me? Certainly not! But sin, that it might appear sin, was producing death in me through what is good, so that sin through the commandment might become exceedingly sinful"* (Romans 7:13). It is after this deep awareness, he concludes, *"I am carnal,"* (Romans 7:14). Here is the core of all sin. It is the *carnal* which is an attitude of self-will and self-sourcing. Even the good deeds that I want to do end up being bad. This so dominates that what I hate is what I produce. No wonder he cries, *"Now if I do what I will not to do, it is no longer I who do it, but sin that dwells in me,"* (Romans 7:20). He summarizes this state in which he exists the *body of death* (Romans 7:24). When I am sourced by Christ, I live; when I source myself, I die. Every attempt I make to affect my own escape from death and to merit life by my achievements is simply another effort to live from myself. This only entangles me the more in sin and therefore death. The law which set out to lead me to life ends up leading me to death.

What a tragic dilemma in which to dwell. How will I ever escape? The best I can do is still filthy rags in His sight and only produces more death. At the close of the chapter Paul breaks into praise for all is not lost! He cries, *"I thank God – through Jesus Christ our Lord!"* (Romans 7:25). He begins the next chapter by saying, *"There is therefore now no condemnation to those who are in Christ Jesus, who do not walk according to the flesh,*

THE PROOF: DEATH IS CONQUERED

but according to the Spirit," (Romans 8:1). He continues by explaining what he means by *walking according to the flesh.* It is a sourcing issue. The flesh in this passage is the carnal self-centered mind. It is man living out of himself. Whenever this takes place, man is dead. But life is produced by the Spirit of Christ sourcing the individual. He says, *"For to be carnally minded is death, but to be spiritually minded is life and peace,"* (Romans 8:6).

CONTINUING DEATH

Death (self-sourcing) is never viewed as simply extinction. Death is not something which takes place when your lungs quit breathing and your heart stops beating. An individual is dead even when eating and breathing. Death is the immediate condition of an individual who is self-sourced. Therefore, death is never viewed as something which happens to an individual and he ceases to exist. Everyone exists forever either in life or in death.

Our culture compartmentalizes everything; it is the way we think. This was not so in the Biblical culture. They thought in terms of the whole; it is what they emphasized. In salvation, we break it into sections such as "saved," "sanctified," "discipleship," and "heaven." The Biblical culture simply thought of "salvation." It was all contained in this one word. This is true of death. We speak of "physical death," "spiritual death," "judgment," and "eternal death (hell). This is not a proper Biblical view. All of these aspects of death exist in the New Testament, but all within the category of death. Paul explained, *"For the wages of sin is death, but the gift of God is*

eternal life in Christ Jesus our Lord," (Romans 6:23).
Obviously Paul was not simply referring to physical death.
He viewed the whole of what happens in an individual
who is sourcing himself.

The Scripture is filled with the progressive revelation
of God. Therefore, one sees this concept developing
through the Old Testament and into the New. Sheol
is a Hebrew word which is normally translated
"grave" (Psalms 88:3, 5). There seems to be two main
compartments to this "abode of the dead." The upper
compartment is referred to as "Paradise" (Luke 23:43).
The lower compartment is called *Hades* (Acts 2:27, 31).
It was believed that all went into this one place, Sheol
(Ecclesiastes 9:2-3). It was a place where love, hate, envy,
work, thought, knowledge, and wisdom were absent
(Ecclesiastes 9:6,10). The atmosphere of such a place
is bleak. There is no light; it is a place of shadows (Job
10:21-22). It would be a place of soul sleeping.

It is strongly presented to us in the New Testament
that something happened to Sheol. There was a drastic
change which altered the construction of the abode of
the dead. The end result was the establishment of heaven
and hell. What was, is no more! When an individual
physically dies, he does not go to Sheol for sleeping, but
is transported directly to heaven or hell. Paul assured
us, *"We are confident, yes, well pleased rather to be
absent from the body and to be present with the Lord,"*
(2 Corinthians 5:8). The Bible does not give us a complete
explanation of what actually took place in the great
transition. We cannot, nor do we want to, be dogmatic.
Rather we are searching and open for truth.

CHRIST – SOLUTION TO DEATH

This we know for certain! Jesus is the answer! A man got us into this mess; it will take a man to get us out of this mess. But where is the man who is not in the mess? The only man who could bring us to life would be one who is not under the domination of death. Obviously God could not find a man who was not controlled by death. Paul said, *"For all have sinned and fall short of the glory of God,"* (Romans 3:23). Of course, *the wages of sin is death* (Romans 6:23). So God decided to become the Man. Christ is the Man who is not controlled by death!

Peter explains Pentecost to the Jews of the Dispersion and to us. He presents the explanation of Jesus. He is the example of what a man filled with the Spirit of God is like. His life was not self-sourced. This would have been sin and therefore death. He was a man who was sourced by God. What was taking place in one hundred and twenty disciples was going on in the person of Christ. The Spirit of life produced life within and through Him. He did not do or live because He was God (although He was and is God). He did what He did because He was a man filled with God.

Since Jesus was not controlled by death, but by the Spirit of life, His death was not the death of a normal man who was already controlled by death. God had to bring Him to death (Acts 2:23). Since sin pays the wages of sin, He had no wages to collect. God made Him to be sin for us. Paul explained, *"For He made Him who knew no sin to be sin for us, that we might become the righteousness of God in Him,"* (2 Corinthians 5:21). God brought Jesus

to death for our sakes. But the same God who brought
Jesus to death has brought Him to life (Acts 2:24). A Man
filled with the Spirit of God went into Sheol, the place of
death and judgment. We have so little information about
the activities which took place there (Ephesians 4:7-10).
What happens when a Man who is being produced and
sourced by the Spirit of God marches into Sheol? It could
not contain Him. Things could not remain the same.
A New Covenant is established. Judgment takes place.
Eternal life is given. No wonder Jesus told us we will
never die (John 11:26).

Death is no longer death for the believer. Paul quotes
Hosea the prophet.

"O Death, where is your sting? O Hades, where is your
victory?" (1 Corinthians 15:55)

He explains that the sting of death is sin
(1 Corinthians 15:56). Sin is found in self-sourcing; self-
sourcing has been eliminated by the sourcing of the Spirit.
Therefore, death no longer has teeth to devour us. It is
the picture presented of Jesus in our passage. He is a Man
filled with the Spirit who has marched into the middle
of death, but death had no way to hold Him. The life
of God sourcing Him was constantly untangling Him.
This happens in all the death entanglements of this life
and in the next. The grasping hold of everything outside
of Christ in this life could not get a grip on Him. The
judgment of death and hell could not contain Him. This
is not because He was God but because He was filled with
God. What happened in Him has also happened in one
hundred and twenty believers and is now promised to
us. We are free in Christ.

11

A Man's Concentration

ACTS 2:25

A great crowd of Jews *from every nation under heaven* are listening intently to Peter's explanation of Pentecost. They earnestly seek an answer to the question, *"Whatever could this mean?"* (Acts 2:12). The Holy Spirit moves on Peter! Cultural environment and tradition have nothing to do with the explanation. This message comes from the heart of God. Peter uses quotes from the Old Testament in a very impressive manner. As he explains the life of Jesus, Peter matches his personal statements with quotes from the Scriptures. There are as many verses dedicated to the statements of Scripture in his message as are dedicated to his personal insights.

Peter begins with the prophecy of Joel (Acts 2:16-21). The one hundred and twenty believers are experiencing an event that God planned and promised for many years. This is the fulfillment of *I will pour out of My Spirit on all flesh* (Acts 2:17). Peter then gives a practical life explanation in the next three verses (Acts 2:22-24). God authenticated the outpouring of the Holy Spirit in *Jesus of Nazareth, a Man.* He did it through the life of Christ, His death, and His resurrection. All that was true of Jesus is now true for us. We have just entered into a new intimacy with God.

Peter bases this thought on a Psalm of David (Psalm 16:8-11). He begins his statement with a Greek word translated *for* (Acts 2:25). It is the Greek word "gar" which is a causative particle. It expresses the reason for what has been. But often this Greek word assumes a reaction on the part of the hearer to what has gone before and gives, in its clause, the reasons for this reaction. No doubt Peter anticipated astonishment from the Jews of the Dispersion. After all, they had been responsible for the crucifixion of Christ. How could they have missed the wonder of what God was doing in this Man? What was taking place in Christ is the highest spiritual reality God has planned for mankind. It is almost to startling to grasp!

What is the basis of this? How could God fill a man, even *Jesus of Nazareth?* They have been carefully looking for the "new thing" which God is going to accomplish. They recognize it in the experience of the one hundred and twenty disciples. How could they have missed it in Christ? How can they now enter into this experience after what they did to Christ?

Peter anticipates their reaction and takes them back to their Scriptures. It is here we clearly see the fundamental truth which opens the possibility of all God wants to do within us. It is found in this Psalm (16:8-11). Above all other Psalms this one is especially considered a "Messianic Psalm." At the original writing of the Psalm, David writes concerning himself. This is the wonder of the Scriptures! God says something through David which goes far beyond the scope of his life. As Peter points out in his sermon, there is absolutely no way this Psalm could apply or be fulfilled in David. Peter says, *"Men and brethren, let me speak freely to you of the patriarch David, that he is both dead and buried, and his tomb is with us to this day,"* (Acts 2:29). Since David is both *dead and buried* among them, this Messianic Psalm could not be about him. It is *Jesus of Nazareth, a Man* in whom this Psalm is fulfilled. The flow of God's life through Christ, which produced His life, His death, and now His resurrection, fulfills the details of this Psalm in every way.

However, there is additional information and details given to us within this quotation of the Psalm. Up to this time the entire focus has been on God who initiated and sourced all that took place in Jesus. But what was the inward spiritual condition which allowed this to happen? How could Jesus maintain this flow of the Holy Spirit in every activity? This seems to be the personal question which we consistently ask. Sometime, at my best moments, I can experience God sourcing me, but how do I maintain this moment by moment? How can I maintain the consistent sourcing of the Spirit of God in my life? This is the most practical aspect of this spiritual reality. We all agree about the power of God, and we certainly embrace the fact that God loves us all. But how do I live in this every day in all situations? What is the key factor which releases this reality within me?

Peter's sermon is an explanation of Pentecost to the Jews of the Dispersion. What is presently in the one hundred and twenty disciples is exactly what was and is within Jesus. What God is doing in and through Jesus is made plain. Now through the statements of David, Peter highlights the attitude present within Jesus which releases this resource. This must be the same attitude or spiritual condition within us, if we are to experience the same sourcing. What is this condition?

Look anew at the quotation of King David: *I foresaw the Lord always before my face, For He is at my right hand, that I may not be shaken* (Acts 2:25).

Remember this is a Messianic Psalm. David is writing these words about himself, but God intended it concerning Christ. With this in mind, it is as if Jesus is speaking these words about Himself.

The Greek word translated *foresaw* must be understood in light of the completed phrase, *always before my face.* This is a strong statement. The strength of the focus cannot be overstated. It is all consuming, all encompassing, and God the Father is appearing in the presence of Jesus. The absolute focus and concentration of *Jesus of Nazareth, a Man* upon His *Lord* (Father) is overpowering; it is as if there is nothing else.

The Greek word translated *before…face* is actually two words combined. The first Greek word would be translated "in." It has the idea of "in, on, at, and by any place or thing, with the major idea of resting." The object is neither moving nor going any place. It is compared with the Greek word "eis" which is translated "into" and implies motion. Another Greek word of comparison is "ek" which is translated "from" which indicates motion out of. Therefore, the Greek word translated *before* actually means "remaining in place." The second Greek word translated *face* can also be translated "eye" or "countenance." The meaning of the statement is that something has come to rest in the very eye, face, or presence of the individual. All of this indicates a strong focus.

This is further emphasized by the Greek word translated *my* which is a part of this same phrase, **before my face.** This Greek word is an emphatic form of me or mine. It is a statement of ownership. Since this is a Messianic Psalm, Jesus states this about Himself. Obviously He refers to His Father. The Father is the object which is in the very eye of Christ without any motion of coming or going. He is the permanent fixture or the remaining vision of Christ. Jesus takes ownership of this focus.

This is further emphasized with the word *always.* It is an interesting translation. This is one of those few places where one English word is the translation for two Greek words. Most often it is the reverse. It is not a compound word, but two different and separate Greek words. The first word is often translated "through," "during," or "with." It implies motion through a place. In our passage, time is the issue. This gives us the meaning of continued time or indefinite time. It can be used in the sense of throughout or during as in "during the whole night," (Luke 5:5), "during forty days," (Acts 1:3). The second word contains the idea of oneness, totality, or the whole. When these two Greek words are used together, the idea of "through the entire time" is conveyed. Thus, we have the translation *always.*

We have a double emphasis on the consistency of what is happening. Something has come to rest in the very eye, face, and presence of Christ. It is consistently there throughout time. Nothing is more valuable to Him. Not even the most startling of events distracts Him. Whenever we come close to Him, this one factor is present. This gives content to the opening statement from our text, *"I foresaw the Lord."*

Do not lose sight of the fact that this is a Messianic Psalm, a statement concerning Christ. The Greek word translated *foresaw* is a compound word. The two words are "before" and "see." It can have the meaning of seeing something before or previously. However, in our passage this verb is in the middle voice. This means that it has to do with personal preference. It means to see before oneself, having before one's eyes, or figuratively, of what one has vividly in mind. This verb is in the indicative mood which means it is a simple statement of fact. There is no argument involved. It is in the imperfect tense. It is an action which took place in the past but continues into the present. This also verifies the continuing action of *always.* The focus of *Jesus of Nazareth, a Man* cannot be questioned. He lives with a constant focus on His Father. His mind is constantly aware (practicing His presence) of the presence of the Father. There is no variation. This is the one fundamental, unchanging, and never-ceasing factor of His life.

In order to be certain we understand the importance of this focus, he adds another key phrase: *For He is at my right hand, that I may not be shaken.* He begins this statement with a conjunction, *for.* It is a different Greek word than found at the beginning of this section (Acts 2:25, see discussion above). This Greek word is most often translated "that" or "because." He gives the basis or reason for his above statement. *Jesus of Nazareth, a Man* is sourced by the very Spirit of God. The spiritual condition which enables this filling is His constant (*always*) focus upon the Father. How is this focus maintained? He is now going to state the reason!

The key to this statement is found in the subject and the verb, *He is*. In the Greek language this is one word. It is the third person singular of the Greek verb translated "to be." He highlights the state of being, not the doing of the Father. The "I am's" of Jesus come from this verb. The focus of Jesus is upon the Father's Person. The Father does not visit Jesus to give Him instruction. It is not during times of great distress that Jesus calls upon the Father and the Father comes to Him. No, Jesus is in intimate relationship with the Father. The presence of the Father (state of being) comes into His very eye, face, and presence. He is not using the Father for His personal advantage. Jesus is not forced to focus on the Father for without Him He will fail. This is not a means to an end. Circumstances cannot affect this focus because it is not about Christ's personal gain. Jesus is captured by the Father, because the Father is actually there. It is a state of being.

Jesus describes it as *at my right hand.* In the ancient world, a bodyguard always stood on the right side of the one he was protecting. In this position he could cover him with his shield and still have his right arm free to fight. The right hand is also mentioned because that was the place of dignity and honor. In our passage, the right hand is used in reference to the entire person. The Father is in the dominant position in relationship to Christ. It is another way of saying what He has already said. The Father has captured the very eye of Christ. The Father is in the very face of Christ until He can see nothing else. No circumstances can get between Christ and the Father. His concentration is stronger than any interference!

There is another important emphasis made in the Greek word translated *at.* The actual Greek word is "ek." The statement is ***He is ek my right hand.*** This Greek word is contrasted with "apo." Both of these Greek words imply motion away from an object. However, "apo" refers distinctly to this motion coming from nearby or around the object, while "ek" always relates to the motion coming from within the object.

This presents two outstanding insights into the concentration of Christ upon His Father. The presence of the Father, while it is a state of being, is also in motion. We should not be surprised concerning this truth. We discover it repeatedly in the Scriptures. Jesus is focused on the Father not because of what the Father is doing, but because of what He is being. However, the state of being is one of great action and accomplishment. The Father's state of being is so powerful it can be described as motion. The energy of the Father's state of being always affects and changes everything around it. The Father defeats every enemy of Christ. It is not a defense of doing, but His very presence defeats the enemy.

This tremendous truth is coupled with the fact that the motion is from within. The action of the state of being is from the very heart or nature of God Himself. The focus of Christ is not upon a facsimile of the Father. Christ is not captured by a portrait or statue of the Father or even ideas about Him. Christ is not focused on an organization or career; this is not theological or conceptual. The Father Himself, state of being, who is in motion within Jesus has absolutely mastered His vision.

Jesus was twelve years of age (Luke 2:42). During the Feast of the Passover His family took Him to Jerusalem.

As they left Jerusalem, they assumed Jesus was in the company with which they were traveling. They had gone an entire day's journey when they realized He was not with them. It took an entire day to return to Jerusalem. They searched another three days for Him throughout the city. In desperation, they went to the temple to seek Divine aid. There He was! They must have been very stern with Him (Luke 2:48). His patient answer was, *"Why did you seek Me? Did you not know that I must be about My Father's business?"* (Luke 2:49). In the Greek text, the word *business* is not there, but is added for clarification in the English. Jesus' statement was, *"Did you not know I must be about My Father?"* Even at age twelve Jesus recognized His dominant focus! It is the Father; His state of existence (*I must be*) was the Father. Nothing else is going on in His life.

This is intimately connected to Peter's explanation of Pentecost. Jesus is the clear and precise explanation of the fullness of the Holy Spirit. He is sourced by the Spirit of the Father. This is maintained consistently because Jesus is totally focused on the Father. The very nature of the Father fills Jesus and sources Him, and it is this same nature which consumes His vision. His very eye becomes filled with the state of being of the Father's presence.

The consistency of the focus of Christ upon the Father allows the constant sourcing of the Holy Spirit. This is highlighted again in the final phrase of our passage. He says, *"that I may not be shaken."* This clause must be seen in the context of Christ's focus on the Father which allows the sourcing. The Messiah must not be shaken from this focus. This must be constant in His life if He is to know the constant resourcing of the Spirit of the Father. What will enable Jesus to maintain this focus? It will not be the power of His mind or discipline. This will not come about because He wills it to be so. The phrase begins with two Greek words translated *that*. It is a phrase consisting of "in order that" or "not." When these are combined it means "in order not," "so that not," or "rest." Why has the Father come in His moving state of being? Why has the Father come to remain in a constant position in the eye of Christ? He does so to keep the focus constant. The One who is responsible for the constant focus is the Father! The Father enables the focus; the Father is the focus; the Father fills and sources the focus. There is no way to be distracted if Jesus responds to the Father.

He climaxes this last clause with *shaken.* In the context of our passage, it expresses the idea of wavering, to move back and forth. It is in the subjunctive mood which suggests a possibility. It is not a certainty, but is desired. The consistent flow of the Holy Spirit sourcing the life of the Messiah is one of focus. It is hopeful that His focus will remain constant, but it is not guaranteed. The Messiah must respond to the Father's presence (state of being), Who has come to be in His eye.

All of this is to explain Pentecost to the Jews of the Dispersion. What has happened in the lives of one hundred and twenty disciples is exactly what was and is taking place in Jesus. He was sourced by the Spirit of God. He lived in total dependence and surrender to the flowing resource of God. How could He maintain this on such a consistent basis? It was because of His focus! His gaze was fixed on the Father. He never wavered from this view. But even this was not produced by His will or determination. The Father came and captured Him. The Father was constantly on His right hand. The Father surrounded, encompassed, and enveloped Him. There was no struggle to remain focused. He relaxed in the presence of the Father and responded to His love.

This is now promised to us! Jesus said, *"As the Father loved Me, I also have loved you; abide in My love,"* (John 15:9). He also said, *"As the living Father sent Me, and I live because of the Father, so he who feeds on Me will live because of Me,"* (John 6:57). Is there anything else needed? Could I respond and rest in Him?

12

A Man's Celebration

ACTS 2:26

Peter is preaching an amazing sermon. It is the explanation of the Pentecost event. The words are coming from his mouth, but the Spirit of God is moving through him, sourcing those words. The Jews of the Dispersion, having just witnessed the Pentecost event, are open and responding to the new thing God is doing through Pentecost. They are eager to know how they too may experience Pentecost just as the one hundred and twenty believers. How can this apply to their lives?

Jesus is the explanation! This is Peter's opening sentence. God proved Pentecost in *Jesus of Nazareth, a Man.* He did it through the life of Jesus, His death, and His resurrection. The focus of the explanation is on sourcing. The essence of the Spirit of God sourced everything which flowed from the being of Christ. The central issue of Pentecost or Christianity is sourcing. It is not about theological correctness, proper behavior, or right versus wrong. It is about sourcing. Who is responsible for what is coming through and from you? Is it coming from you or through and from the Spirit of God?

Peter is very much aware that this kind of statement will produce a reaction. Certain questions will be raised. How can this happen in my life? If I experience Pentecost, how will I maintain a consistent sourcing of the Spirit? He forcibly says the answer is still found in Jesus. He quotes to us a Messianic Psalm (Psalm 16:8-11). This passage can easily be broken into three sections. These three sections combined give us the secret of how *Jesus of Nazareth, a Man* maintained on a consistent basis the sourcing of the Spirit of God even in and through death. The three sections are **CONCENTRATION** (Acts 2:25), **CELEBRATION** (Acts 2:26), and **COMMUNION** (Acts 2:27-28).

Jesus' concentration was completely on the Father. This is a Messianic Psalm. This means we must take these words as those of Christ. He boldly says that the Father is in His eye. His entire vision is the Father. The Father is so large in His eyesight that Jesus can see nothing else. This vision is not a picture of the Father, ideas about the Father, or a statue of the Father. The actual Father, in the essence of His Spirit is present. His very presence acts like a body guard which defeats every enemy. Jesus is able to maintain this vision of His Father because of the Father. He does not have special discipline, techniques, or meditation methods. It is the Father Himself who sources the consistency. As Jesus sees the Father, He is captured by Him. Because He is captured by the Father, He consistently sees the Father. The very presence of the Father sources the consistency. Jesus is simply responding to the Father. Remember this is an explanation of Pentecost. What is happening in Jesus is now transferred to the disciples. This is also promised to us. This is the key to our lives as well.

The overflow of this is **CELEBRATION** (Acts 2:26). This seems to describe the tone of the response which is constantly going on in the life of *Jesus of Nazareth, a Man.*

Therefore my heart rejoiced and my tongue was glad; Moreover my flesh also will rest in hope (Acts 2:26).

He begins with the Greek word translated *therefore.* There are two Greek words which are translated into this one English word. The first Greek word is the same as in the above study for the Greek word translated *always.* It is a primary preposition denoting the channel of an act, through, or during. It implies motion, through a place. The second Greek word can be translated "that thing." So a proper translation beginning this great statement would be "through that thing." What was the constant attitude present through the concentration (Acts 2:25)? If Jesus lived in a total focus on the Father, He was in His eye, what was happening in the inner life of Christ through it all?

The Messiah seems to realize that His life is filled with "rejoicing." *Rejoiced* is a translation of a compound Greek word. The first word is "well" and the second one is "mind." This is an entirely different Greek word than what Paul uses in Philippians as he instructs us to *Rejoice in the Lord always. Again I will say, rejoice!* (Philippians 4:4). Paul uses the same Greek word Jesus used in the Sermon on the Mount concerning persecution. *"Rejoice and be exceedingly glad, for great is your reward in heaven,"* (Matthew 5:12). However, the Greek word Peter is using here in quoting David is only used fourteen times in the New Testament. Six of those times it is translated "merry." It is an interesting word because it is a verb used in the context of relationship. It is used strongly in the Parable of the Prodigal Son. Upon the return of the son, the fatted calf was killed and a party was given. Jesus said, *"And they began to be merry,"* (Luke 15:24). The elder brother accused the Father by saying, *"You never gave me a young goat, that I might make merry with my friends,"* (Luke 15:29). It has the connotation of having a party with one's friends. Paul makes the use of this word plain in asking a question, *For if I make you sorrowful, then who is he who makes me glad* (merry) *but the one who is made sorrowful by me?* (2 Corinthians 2:2). Since this Greek word has to do with relationship, it becomes very important in regard to intimacy with God. The chief sin in one's relationship to God is denial of God as the cause of joy. When I depend upon circumstances, materialism, or power to determine my merriment, I have sinned. In Stephen's great message to the Jews he related the story of the golden calf. He said, *"And they made a calf in those days, offered sacrifices to the idol, and rejoiced in the works of their own hands"* (Acts 7:41). The golden calf was not their only sin, but they had shifted the cause of their joy to something other than God.

This becomes significant in the context of our passage concerning *Jesus of Nazareth, a Man.* It was through those things such as His life and His death that the focus on His Father strengthened. In the context of His relationship with the Father, there was a "well mind." He lived in dependence on the flow of the indwelling Spirit. This brought the spirit of merriment. It took place in His *heart.* It is exciting to see that the usage of this word in the New Testament does not depend upon the Greek concept or usage of the word but is influenced by the Old Testament. It refers to the inner person. It is the seat of understanding, knowledge, and will. It takes on the meaning of conscience. It is described most effectively by Peter in his challenge to wives. He calls them to something beyond *merely outward* adornment – *arranging the hair, wearing gold, or putting on fine apparel – rather let it be the hidden person of the heart, with the incorruptible beauty of a gentle and quiet spirit, which is very precious in the sight of God* (1 Peter 3:3-4). *The hidden person of the heart* describes well the New Testament concept of *heart.*

In our passage, *therefore my heart rejoiced, heart* is the subject and *rejoiced* is the verb. It is interesting this verb is in the passive voice. This means the *heart* is not responsible for the merriment. This is not a matter of getting oneself into a positive mental state. We are not being challenged to discipline our thought process to blot out all negative thoughts. The *hidden person of the heart* of the Messiah is being acted upon by the very relationship of intimacy with the Father. He is living in a party, making merriment. But He is being brought to death! Yes, it is a death *delivered by the determined purpose and foreknowledge of God.* Even in death, the relationship is intimate and flowing in merriment.

The next clause in our passage is most exulting. *Jesus of Nazareth, a Man* exclaims, *"and my tongue was glad;"* (Acts 2:26). The Greek word translated *tongue* can mean the organ of the body or often it stands for speech or language. The Greek word translated *was glad* is a compound word. The first Greek word means "much;"

127

the second Greek word means "to leap." Therefore, this Greek word means "to leap for joy, to show one's joy by leaping and skipping." This kind of activity denotes excessive or ecstatic joy and delight. Often in the Old Testament Septuagint this Greek word is used to speak of rejoicing with song and dance (Psalms 2:11; 20:5; 40:16; 68:3). This verb is normally found in the middle voice which has to do with personal preference. He is not expressing a quiet spirit of contentment. This is not resting as in napping. This is a party where things are getting out of hand. Merriment is taking place with my best friend, the God who is sourcing me. It is an occasion to dance on the table, blow party whistles, and play loud music! I just cannot help myself!

Both verbs, *rejoiced* and *was glad*, are in the aorist tense. It adds a timeless element to His condition. This corresponds to the Hebrew perfect tense as found in the original writing in the Psalms. As focus upon the Father is *always* present in His life, so also is the jubilant merriment. Do you see the interworking of these two concepts?

Peter is describing and explaining the Pentecost event. The explanation is Jesus! That which flowed in and through Jesus is now happening in the disciples. This is promised to you. Here is what you can expect when you are filled with the Spirit. When God sources you, look for these things. Jesus will be your total vision. Not because you refuse to see anything else, but because you cannot see anything else. You are captured by Him. You see Him, therefore He captures you. Since you are captured by Him, you see Him. This produces in your inner person a merriment which is not affected by circumstances, pressures, or even death!

The next major phrase in the Messiah's statement is just as startling. He says, *"Moreover my flesh also will rest in hope"* (Acts 2:26). *Moreover* literally means "the continuation of a condition or action." It can also mean "in addition, further, or besides." How could there be anything more? To experience all we have just proposed would be more than one could expect in a multitude of lifetimes. It only points us to the abundance of His presence when flowing through *a Man.* There seems to be no end to the extravagant benefits.

It is very valuable for us to grasp the full significance of the reference to *my flesh.* The actual Greek word does refer to the physical body as distinguished from the spirit or soul. Many scholars believe this statement in our verse is in regard to the hope of the resurrection. Peter has just preached about the Spirit of God producing the death of Christ. Now he quotes the Messianic Psalm in which the Messiah is expressing His hope and trust in God who will raise Him from the dead. However, there is room for a larger and deeper interpretation than this.

In the preceding statement the Messiah has revealed the joy and merriment within His *heart* and *tongue.* We discovered the *heart* is the *hidden person of the heart.* This joy is a condition of the inner most person which certainly affects the flesh but is not dependent upon it. The Greek word translated *tongue* can most definitely refer to the organ in the body. As stated above, it can also refer to speech or language. However, David originally wrote this in the Hebrew language. In the original Psalm the Hebrew word is actually translated *glory.* It expresses the idea of abundance, honor, and dignity. This Hebrew word expresses the glory of God filling the temple. This would not be a focus on the physical presence of God, but the Spirit and essence of His presence. Peter, in quoting this Psalm, followed the translation of the Septuagint rather than the Hebrew text. In this change the translators shifted from the glory (Hebrew) to the tongue (Greek). In light of the total statement, the Messiah is expressing the condition of the inner person (*heart*). What is being expressed is not just from the physical tongue but from the very soul, being, or essence of His existence.

With this in clear focus, we must view the statement of *my flesh* as an expression of something beyond the physical body. This is not a statement of the confidence the Messiah has in the physical resurrection from the dead. As we have understood from Peter's sermon, the resurrection is more than an event. It is not just a physical resurrection of the body, although that is included. The resurrection is a state of being which flows from the indwelling and sourcing of the Spirit of God within the individual. So the idea of *flesh* in this verse must be seen as greater than just the physical. It represents the entire person.

This is further seen in a proper understanding of the concept of *will rest in hope*. The Greek word translated *will rest* literally means to dwell in a tent or tabernacle, to camp. This Greek word is used by Jesus in the Parable of the Mustard Seed. He tells us of the smallest seed the Jews possessed which grows into the largest tree in their land. It *becomes a tree, so that the birds of the air come and nest in its branches* (Matthew 13:32). This portrays the idea of lodging or remaining. The birds do not simply alight temporarily in the tree but nest and permanently dwell.

Jesus of Nazareth, a Man says, "*Moreover my flesh*

also will rest in hope." Some scholars have interpreted this to be an expression of the Messiah's faith. He could yield His flesh to death in confidence of the physical resurrection. So *hope* is the resting place, the camping site, or the permanent dwelling of His flesh in death. However, in understanding *flesh* as more than the physical body we begin to perceive a deeper meaning of this statement. *Hope* is not the place of dwelling, but literally means "as may be hoped." The place of dwelling is His focus on the Father.

The Messiah said in the beginning of Peter's quotation (Acts 2:26) that the Father was in His eye. This vision is so dominant, He cannot see anything else. No circumstances or difficulties are able to distract Him. This focus on the Father is absolutely consistent. This is not a picture of the Father, and it is not an idea or doctrine of the Father. The actual essence of the life of the Father has come to be His body guard. This means because He is seeing the Father He is consistently focused on the Father. Therefore, the Father is producing or sourcing the focus. Jesus is simply responding to the stimuli of the Father's presence. This produces merriment in the depths of His inner being. It is so strong it permeates His entire life even to the physical body. Since His entire being, both spiritually and physically dwells, permanently lodges, rests, or nests in this focus, He may continue to hope in the Father. The Messiah will continue to live in the fullness of the Father. What the Father has been doing within Him, the Father will continue to do through Him. The unseen future holds no fear because of the dwelling place of the focus on the Father.

Peter is explaining Pentecost. Pentecost is Christianity.

The Old Covenant is now gone and the New Covenant is present. *Christ in you* is now ours (Colossians 1:27). As the Father sourced Jesus, so Jesus now wants to source us. How can this be maintained on a moment by moment basis? The key is in the focus. We must focus on Jesus as Jesus focused on the Father (Acts 2:25). You and I can experience this same focus which takes place in the same sourcing of the Spirit. This will produce the same jubilant merriment which Jesus experienced in relationship with the Father. This sourcing can permeate our lives until He is our lodging place. We can live in the eternal hope of this focus and sourcing continues forever. Even in crucifixion there is no fear. The life both physically and spiritually is consumed by the focus of His presence. Christ is ours; we are His!

A Man's Communion

ACTS 2:27

Peter, filled with the Holy Spirit, is being used by God to explain to the Jews of the Dispersion the outpouring of the Spirit of Christ. His explanation is for us as well. He focuses his explanation on Jesus. In order to understand Pentecost, we must understand Jesus. *Jesus of Nazareth, a Man* was the proof of Pentecost. God sourced this *Man* so all could see and understand the full potential God intends for mankind. God sourced the life of Christ (Acts 2:22), the death of Christ (Acts 2:23), and the resurrection of Christ (Acts 2:24).

What was the spiritual condition of Jesus which allowed this sourcing? Furthermore, how did Jesus maintain this sourcing moment by moment? To answer these questions, Peter reverts back to the Old Testament Scriptures. There must not be any chance of misunderstanding. This is not Peter's opinion, cultural perspective, or memorized answer. The explanation comes from King David who speaks concerning the Messiah (Acts 2:25). It is a quotation from a Messianic Psalm (Psalms 16:8-11).

The Father sourced Jesus because of His spiritual condition. The key element was Christ's focus. The **CONCENTRATION** of Christ was on the Father (Acts 2:25). The Father appeared in the eye of Christ until He could see nothing else. The Father is the source of the concentration as Christ responds to His appearance. As the Son sees the Father, He loves Him. As Jesus loves the Father, He is driven to see Him. As Jesus sees the Father, He loves Him. This drives Jesus to see Him. The very presence of the Father perpetuates the concentration.

This produces a condition of **CELEBRATION** within the inner most person of Christ (Acts 2:26). There is a merriment which resembles a party flowing between the Father and Son. It affects the entire being of Christ which enables Him to have hope. The very dwelling place of the Spirit filled Man is the presence of the Father. This fullness enables Him to hope in all situations, even His death and resurrection.

Then the Messiah breaks into an outburst of this celebration (Acts 2:27). It is an expression of worship as the Son actually speaks to the Father. The Messiah is giving details of the depth of the **COMMUNION** which takes place between them in the fullness of the Holy Spirit. Remember this is an explanation of Pentecost. Everything true of *Jesus of Nazareth, a Man* is taking place in the one hundred and twenty disciples. It is also promised to you.

The beginning statement of this worship is *"For You will not leave my soul in Hades,"* (Acts 2:27). This statement is so important and powerful that Peter restates it as he continues preaching. He interprets this statement in light of the promise of the Father to King David (Acts 2:30).

It is a validation of the resurrection of the Messiah according to Peter: *"he, foreseeing this, spoke concerning the resurrection of the Christ, that His soul was not left in Hades, nor did His flesh see corruption,"* (Acts 2:31). This is an Old Testament statement of the New Testament reality proposed in verse twenty-four. God was proving Pentecost in *Jesus of Nazareth, a Man.* One of the proofs was found in the resurrection. *A Man* filled with the Spirit could not be contained in death. Death is pictured as long, gigantic fingers reaching to seize, capture, and imprison the individual. He gives the picture of a baby trapped in his mother's womb. Death can no more hold the person filled with the Spirit than a pregnant woman can keep her baby in her womb. When one is filled with the Spirit, he can move into the midst of death with complete freedom from fear. Death is anything which is not sourced by the Spirit. All the aspects of death connected to daily living fall by the wayside. They try to entangle us, but it is not allowed because of the Spirit of Christ. The seizing fingers of death slide from the believer. This is also true for death as contained in physical and eternal death. Jesus told us, *"And whoever lives and believes in Me shall never die. Do you believe this?"* (John 11:26). The reason for the truth of this statement is the intimacy of the fullness of the Spirit. Death is no longer death. The sting has been removed. Evidently there is something so powerful and explosive within the relationship of the Spirit of Christ and the believer that death is no longer a threat!

The depth of the relationship producing this reality is expressed in the verb of the opening sentence of our passage. It is *will (not) leave. Leave* is a combination of two Greek words. These two words can be translated "in" and "forsake, abandon, or desert." It means to "leave behind in any state or place." Jesus is obviously speaking of His Father who is in His eye.

The Messiah's proclamation is strong; the Father will not abandon or leave Him. The intertwining of the Father and the Son is so tight that there is no possibility of separation. There is a complete unity between them. They cannot be divided even by death. It is the picture of the vine and the branch relationship (John 15). The two are distinct yet not the same; but they are so united you cannot see where one leaves off and the other begins. This is the man filled with the Spirit of Christ. Peter is explaining Pentecost. The fullness of the Holy Spirit is a state of intimacy with Christ. It is so tight and complete He cannot go off and leave you.

We must carefully investigate this key word. The Greek word translated *leave* (engkataleipo) is actually a compound word. The first Greek word is "en" which is used numerous times in the New Testament. The second Greek word is "kataleipo." This word is used twenty-four times in the New Testament. It means "to forsake, abandon, or leave behind." One would think this word (kataleipo) would have been adequate to express the cry of the Messiah's heart in our passage. But when Peter quoted this Psalm, he used the Greek word "engkataleipo." This states the basic idea of forsaking or leaving behind, but strengthens the relational aspect of the statement.

Let us review the use of the Greek word "en." You may remember from previous studies the role this word plays in comparison with "into" (eis) and "from" (ek). Both of these words indicate motion either away from or towards. But the word "in" has no motion. It bespeaks the fact of

136

resting, remaining, or abiding. In the New Testament this word is used in regard to a person being filled with something. Sin is not a simple deed, but actually lives in a person (Romans 7:17-20). The opposite of this is God's Spirit living within the believer (Romans 8:9-11; 1 Corinthians 3:16). Life, joy, faith, and the Word are said to be in people because of the presence of the Spirit of Christ (John 6:53, 15:11; 2 Timothy 1:5; John 5:38). *All the treasures of wisdom and knowledge* are found in Christ (Colossians 2:3). The mystery and the life are both hidden in God (Ephesians 3:9; Colossians 3:3).

Most important for us is the use of this word for the inner relationship between God and a person. There are frequent statements that God actually works in a person (1 Corinthians 12:6; Philippians 1:6, 2:13; Colossians 1:29). Paul seems to present a formula which he emphatically states as *Christ in you* (Romans 8:10; 2 Corinthians 13:5; Colossians 1:27). This description was highlighted by Jesus in the upper room discourse on the promise of the Father (John 14, 15, and 16). In describing His own relationship with the Father He said, *"Believe Me that I am in the Father and the Father in Me,"* (John 14:11). He continued, *"I am in My Father, and you in Me, and I in you,"* (John 14:20). In describing the coming experience of the fullness of the Spirit, Jesus said, *"He dwells with you and will be in you,"* (John 14:17).

This gives us a good understanding of the use of "in" (en). Remember this is the first of two words combined together in the Greek word translated *leave* (engkataleipo) in our text (Acts 2:27). The second word (kataleipo) is really interesting for it is also a compound word. It is the Greek word which can be translated "down," and the

Greek word which can be translated "forsake" or "leave." The first Greek word translated "down" can mean "down from," "down upon," or "down in." It has the connotation of "deep throughout." This second Greek word translated "forsake" or "leave" can mean "fail," "wanting," or "deficient."

If this has become clear in your thinking, you are automatically asking a question. Why would they place the word "in" (en) at the beginning of the word "leave" (kataleipo) and form a whole new word (engkataleipo)? Clearly something distinctive is being stated by the use of this word. This is not about simply leaving something behind as in leaving a message, but has to do with relationship. This Greek word (engkataleipo) is used ten times in the New Testament. Each time it is used there is relationship involved. It is the word used in the statement of Christ on the cross when He cried out, *"My God, My God, why have You forsaken Me?"* (Matthew 27:46; Mark 15:34). Paul also used this same term in referring to Demas. He said, *"Be diligent to come to me quickly; for Demas has forsaken me, having loved this present world, and has departed for Thessalonica"* (2 Timothy 4:9-10).

In this Messianic Psalm, the Messiah is giving us deep insight into the intimacy and oneness found in the fullness of the Spirit. The Father is in the eye of the Son. This is not an acquaintance relationship. This is not a mutually beneficial relationship. This is not even a need based relationship. The unity is deep in the fullness of the Spirit; there is no possibility of separation. The security of the relationship is found in unity and oneness. There is no deficiency even in the realm of the dead. This relationship supersedes every circumstance of life and death.

This concept is even further expanded by the direct object of the verb. Jesus says, *"For you will not leave my soul in Hades."* The focus of the action of the verb is on the direct object, *my soul.* This was startling to me. Perhaps I have had the wrong interpretation of *soul.* When *soul* is suggested, I immediately think of the part of my being which is in the image of God. It is the spiritual aspect of my life where God intends to indwell. This interpretation is not what Jesus is saying in our verse. The Greek word translated *soul* has to do with "the principle of life." It is contrasted with physical death. This Greek word can be used for both man and animals.

An example can be found in the story of a man who fell asleep in church. Let this be a warning to all who might be tempted to do this. Paul is preaching. A man falls asleep while sitting in a window. He falls three stories to the ground and dies. *But Paul went down, fell on him, and embracing him said, "Do not trouble yourselves, for his life* (soul) *is in him"* (Acts 20:10). So this Greek word translated *soul* is used in the New Testament to refer to the natural life existence of men. It becomes a word which encompasses the essence of my existence. Thus, it is used in our passage. The Messiah is saying that the intimacy He has with the Father is so strong that who He is cannot be separated from the Father. The Father has become the heart of His DNA. The Father is not a warm jacket Jesus wears. The Father is the center ingredient of every cell of Christ's being. There is no way to separate the Father from who He is. Any attempt of separation would destroy Him. It would be easier to remove the mother's or father's genetic makeup from their child than to separate the Father from the life principle of Jesus.

We must see this in the context of Peter's explanation of Pentecost. The Father is sourcing Jesus. The spiritual condition of Jesus which allows this is the consistent concentration on the Father. The Father has gotten into the eye of the Messiah, and Jesus has responded to this vision. This has produced merriment (party) between these two with the undercurrent of the absolute confidence of hope. The communion is so strong between them; there is no possibility of separation. Not even **Hades** (the realm of the dead) can disturb this party of unity. If one can experience a party with the Spirit of the Father in **Hades**, what could be the circumstances which could separate us from Him? The Messiah is describing the depth of the communion found in the fullness of the Spirit!

The second phrase in our passage is just as intriguing. It says, *"Nor will You allow Your Holy One to see corruption,"* (Acts 2:27). Here is a bold statement of confidence in relationship. The verb *will allow* is a Greek word which focuses on source. It comes from the Greek word "didomi" and means "to give or bestow upon." This word is the most common expression for the procedure whereby a subject deliberately transfers something to someone or something so that it becomes available to the recipient. In our sentence, it is in the negative. The Father who is in the eye of the Messiah and with whom there is a depth of communion and unity WILL NOT GIVE corruption to the One who is filled with the Spirit.

Let us examine the logic of the total picture found here. Peter is explaining Pentecost to the Jews of the Dispersion. Jesus is the explanation. He is a man who is sourced by the Father. Everything He has is given to Him by the Father. His life with all of its aspects is sourced by the

Father. Even Jesus' death is given to Him by the Father. His resurrection is certainly a gift of the Father. Jesus is totally dependent upon the Father for every function. The spiritual condition within Jesus which allows this sourcing is His absolute concentration on the Father. The Father is in His eye. Jesus simply responds to the Father which strengthens the focus. This produces merriment (party) within the relationship. Hope and confidence flow from this intimacy. This relationship is so intimate separation is impossible without the destruction of who Jesus is. The Father has become the DNA of the essence of Christ. It is so strong it can exist even in the realm of death. The absolute certainty of this is found in the sourcing of the Father. The Father would never source the Son with corruption. The Father is life and light. The Father will never give the Son destruction, damnation, or corruption. If this is true in Jesus, it is true in us through the fullness of the same Spirit. Obviously the key is found in the total sourcing of the Spirit of God.

This is further highlighted by the Greek word translated *to see.* It is not simply to physically see. It means to perceive, grasp, understand, or know. It has an inward focus. This is especially important when we attempt to comprehend the meaning of *corruption.* Many Bible scholars interpret this word to refer to the physical body of Jesus. They specifically relate this to the decaying of the body of Christ during His three days in the grave. They are very strong in declaring that Jesus' body did not experience any form of returning to dust. When the blood stops circulating to the cells of the body, the decaying process begins in the body. Some believe this did not happen to Christ. I have not been able to embrace this concept! It violates the focus of Peter's sermon. Peter is explaining Pentecost. Jesus is the complete explanation or example of the content of Pentecost. What happened to Jesus is taking place in the one hundred and twenty disciples, and is promised to you. This would mean I would not need to be embalmed when I die for my body will never experience decay. But that is not true. Peter expresses that it was not even true for King David (Acts 2:29).

However, the main difficulty is basing this truth on this passage and especially the Greek word translated *corruption.* This same word is used by Luke in his Gospel account. Jesus is instructing His disciples not to worry. He said, *"Sell what you have and give alms; provide yourselves money bags which do not grow old, a treasure in the heavens that does not fail, where no thief approaches nor moth destroys* (Luke 12:33). In the revelation of the second trumpet in the Book of the Revelation, we see the same word. *And a third of the living creatures in the sea died, and a third of the ships were destroyed* (Revelation 8:9). In our text in the Book of Acts, one must see this word in this same way. The focus is not on the body not decaying, but upon the entire destructive power of death (*Hades*). The focus is on the liberation from the destruction that is brought about by death. This is further verified in Paul's sermon when he said, *"And that He raised Him from the dead, no more to return to corruption,"* (Acts 13:34).

The Messiah is once again declaring the depth of intimacy found in the communion of the fullness of the Holy Spirit. There is no chance of destruction for the one who is filled with the Spirit of Christ. The core of every cell of his being is throbbing with the life of God. The intimacy is so deep He will not abandon the believer, nor give him destruction. Our total confidence and hope is found here. As this was experienced by Jesus, so this is now promised to us. The oneness Jesus had with the Father, we are now to experience with Him. Every circumstance of life must be faced with the awareness of His presence. He will not abandon us nor give us destruction!

14

A MAN'S COMMUNICATION

ACTS 2:28

Jesus' inner heart is full of worship. He is giving wonderful expression to that worship in a Messianic Psalm. He moves from CONCENTRATION (Acts 2:25) to CELEBRATION (Acts 2:26). This produces a change in language from speaking about His Father to actually addressing Him in worship. There is a COMMUNION (Acts 2:27) expressed in His worship. The Father and Son have become one. They cannot be separated. There is a COMMUNICATION established. The Son cries, *"You have made known to me the ways of life;"* (Acts 2:28).

The communication level between the Messiah and the Father who has filled Him is very strong. This does not surprise you. It matches the level of the intimacy between them. There is correspondence between intimacy and communication. One must not think there can be barriers and communication will still take place. If I am not hearing clearly, I may not be embracing properly. The intimacy level must be the beginning place of correction.

This is highlighted in His opening statement in verse twenty-eight. *You have made known* is a translation of one Greek word. It is used twenty-five times in the New Testament. It is completely beyond the idea of "to say." It is not on the level of a simple conversation. It is not the equivalent of writing someone a note. In the New Testament this has to do with announcing. It is blaring, even bold. It means "to make known publicly or explicitly." If one investigates the appearance of this Greek word in the New Testament (twenty-five times), they all relate to God or the salvation event in Christ.

In our passage, the level of communication must be understood far beyond yelling or shouting the information. He is not necessarily saying that God, the Father, forcefully informed Him. It has to do with communication derived from intimacy. For instance, there is a communication level unique to husband and wife. It comes from years of intimacy. It is beyond verbal statements. Some men call it "the look." One just knows how the other feels or thinks. This depth of communication is present between Jesus and His Father. The Father is able to share the depth of His heart and passion. But not only is the Father able to share it, the Son is able to grasp it. It comes from the intimacy they have together. In our relationships with each other, there are very few people with whom you can share everything. You say to that person, "I can't tell this to anyone else. They just would not understand." This person understands because you have shared many experiences together, some of overwhelming joy and some of incredible sorrow. You share on a very intimate level. The Father is revealing the depth of life to the Son. This happens because they have become one.

You must constantly remember this entire discussion concerns the explanation of Pentecost. Jesus is the explanation for the fullness of the Spirit. He is sourced by the Father. What takes place within Him is now happening in one hundred and twenty disciples, and it is promised to you and me. This sourcing of the Father comes because of the spiritual condition of Jesus. He is totally concentrated on the Father. The Father is in His eye (Acts 2:25). This produces an amazing celebration (Acts 2:26). It is on the level of high-spirited fun which takes place between the Father and the Son. Out of this comes worship which is an expression of the depth of the communion they experience together (Acts 2:27). It is impossible to separate them. Even death cannot untangle who the Father is from who Jesus is. Now we see the wonder of the communication happening between them (Acts 2:28). This is all taking place within the experience of Pentecost. This is no longer unique to Jesus, but was given to the disciples and now to you and me.

Jesus must have spent hours with the disciples in the upper room explaining this (John 14, 15 and 16). He attempted to get them ready for His death, resurrection, and ascension. They were deeply troubled because He kept speaking of His departure. They could not imagine life without Him. How could He describe this to them? He said, *"No longer do I call you servants, for a servant does not know what his master is doing; but I have called you friends, for all things that I heard from My Father I have made known to you"* (John 15:15). Jesus used the same Greek word as found in our text. To move from a servant to a friend is a shift in intimacy. In the context of this intimacy Jesus is now communicating to us. It is Pentecost.

Paul was deeply aware of this reality. He had experienced both the old and new covenants. Of all his contemporaries he has been the most zealous for the traditions of the fathers (Galatians 1:14). He had lived in the mystery of the Old Testament. It was a shadow in which the revelation had *been hidden from ages and from generations, but now has been revealed to His saints* (Colossians 1:26). The revelation of the hidden mystery is very simple, yet it is immersed in riches and glory. Here is what has been revealed to the saints. *To them God willed to make known what are the riches of the glory of this mystery among the Gentiles: which is Christ in you, the hope of glory* (Colossians 1:27). Paul uses the same Greek word found in our text. Think of the intimacy found in *the riches of the glory of this mystery!* Christ is in you. This is the hope of glory. This is the intimacy level which enables Christ to make Himself known to us.

The Book of Ephesians is such a powerful treatment of what is happening in the unseen world. Paul begins by declaring that God has spoken into being every good thing He wants us to have (Ephesians 1:3). He has placed them all in Christ. He then begins to list these great blessings. It is only a partial list, but it is completely overwhelming. He has chosen us. He has adopted us. Holiness is ours. We have become accepted. Redemption is ours through His blood. He has given the *riches of His grace which He made to abound toward us in all wisdom and prudence, having made known to us the mystery of His will, according to His good pleasure which He purposed in Himself,* (Ephesians 1:7-9). The Greek word in our text appears again. The intimacy level of being in Christ, accepted in the Beloved, enables a communication beyond knowledge. It is what is *purposed in Himself.* We know the mind of Christ.

Let us return to our passage in Acts. *You have made known to me the ways of life;* (Acts 2:28). It appears the most effective way to grasp the meaning of *life* is to see it in the context of the ministry of Jesus. In ministering to Nicodemus, Jesus spoke of being lifted up like a serpent in the wilderness. The purpose of which was *"whoever believes in Him should not perish but have eternal LIFE"* (John 3:15). *"For God so loved the world that He gave His only begotten Son, that whoever believes in Him should not perish but have everlasting LIFE"* (John 3:16). The conclusion is simply stated by John the Baptist. *"He who believes in the Son has everlasting LIFE, and he who does not believe the Son shall not see LIFE; but the wrath of God abides on him"* (John 3:36). Jesus continued in ministry by speaking to a Samaritan woman. He offered her water and said, *"But the water that I shall give him will become in him a fountain of water springing up into everlasting LIFE"* (John 4:14). Jesus pleaded with the people of His day, *"Do not labor for the food which perishes, but for the food which endures to everlasting LIFE, which the Son of Man will give you,"* (John 6:27). In speaking about Himself, Jesus said, *"For the bread of God is He who comes down from heaven and gives LIFE to the world"* (John 6:33). The crowd responded with a desire for this bread. Jesus continued, *"I am the bread of LIFE"* (John 6:35). In the same discourse Jesus declared, *"And this is the will of Him who sent Me, that everyone who sees the Son and believes in Him may have everlasting LIFE;"* (John 6:40). The crowd began to complain about His statements. Jesus continued to clarify, *"Most assuredly, I say to you, he who believes in Me has everlasting LIFE. I am the bread of LIFE,"* (John 6:47-48). In further explanation Jesus said, *"I am the LIVING bread which came down from heaven. If anyone eats of this bread, he will LIVE forever; and the bread that I shall give is My flesh, which I shall give for the LIFE of the world"* (John 6:51). You can do further research yourself to see how Jesus used this Greek word.

Life was used in early Christianity to characterize salvation. The Old Testament shows a strong contrast between the dead gods of the world and the Living God. The actions of our God prove He is alive. The dead gods were manufactured by the hands of men. Men had to take care of these gods. They were served, protected, and given provisions. Our Living God is one who acts in our behalf. He delivers us. The Old Testament contains the abundant stories of the great deliverances of our Living God in our behalf. This is the Living God who is sourcing *Jesus of Nazareth, a Man.* His sourcing is one of LIFE. Whatever is contained in this word is flowing through Jesus to His world. This is what has now possessed the hundred and twenty disciples. This is what is promised to you and me!

There is a significant connection between the LIFE and the "way." It seems to be at the very heart of the communication between the Father and the Son. This communication is far beyond the sharing of data or information. It is completely outside the realm of drawing Him a map or showing Him a path. This seems to be the danger in referring to Christianity as a journey. We immediately think of the Bible as a road map. We study carefully to make the right turns and stay on the correct way. While this symbolism is valid we must constantly be aware of the danger it suggests.

Perhaps the author of the Book of Hebrews clarifies it. Here is his declaration: ***"Therefore, brethren, having boldness to enter the Holiest by the blood of Jesus, by a new and LIVING WAY which He consecrated for us, through the veil, that is, His flesh, and having a High Priest over the house of God,"*** (Hebrews 10:19-21). I was really intrigued by the use of the word ***boldness***. This is translated from a compound Greek word. It is the words "all" and "the act of speaking." It is used to express freedom or frankness in speaking all that one thinks or pleases. This describes Jesus as He was relating the first prediction of His death and resurrection. ***He spoke this word openly*** (Mark 8:32). Especially in Hebrews and First John the word denotes confidence which is connected with communion with God through Christ. This new communication enables us ***to enter into the Holiest.*** The Greek word translated ***to enter*** is a compound word. It is the combination of "into" (eis) and "way" (same Greek word in Acts 2:28). An astonishing embrace has happened in Christ. We have been given the ability to communicate on a whole new level to the extent it has placed us into a new way.

What has made this possible? The Hebrew author cries out, "It is ***by a new and living way,"*** (Hebrews 10:20). The Greek word translated ***new*** as used in this verse is significant. This is the only time it is used in the entire New Testament. It is like God saved this word for a special emphasis as related to Christ. Its original meaning was "freshly slaughtered." Jesus is the new way, the freshly slaughtered sacrifice. He opens the new communication level to God. What seems odd is for the Hebrew author to continue to call this death sacrifice the *living way*. The *living way* is the cross way. He continues to clarify that the *way* was *consecrated for us* by Christ. The Greek word translated *consecrated* is a compound word. "In" and "to make new" are the meaning of the two words. He is pictured as the High Priest who has been freshly slaughtered for the purpose of taking us through the veil right into communication with the heart and mind of God. He is the *living way.* Through intimacy (communication) with Him, we have intimacy (communication) with the Father.

Let us return to our passage in Acts. *You have made known to me the ways of life* (Acts 2:28). This is a good time to review. *You have made known to me* is not in the realm of data or information. It is in the embrace of personal intimacy. Between the Father and the Son is a level of oneness that allows the Son to grasp the inner heart of the Father. The depth of the communication is directly tied to the depth of the intimacy. This same depth is promised to us. It is not academic achievement but the intimacy of Pentecost. The outside God has come inside. In the oneness of the fullness of the Spirit a new level of communication has taken place. In this embrace *the ways of life* are shared. We might have expressed this as "revealed," "comprehended," or "made plain." However, these words miss the intent. They indicate separation or mastering the material. This intimacy is the sharing of the minds until we know, not because we have learned, although there is a maturing process. It is not because we have spiritual disciplines, although He has been disciplining our lives. It is because we have been embraced by Him in oneness.

This is expressed in the word **ways**. It is important to note in the original Psalm (Psalm 16:11) this appears as singular. We must not approach this as if there are several possibilities; rather there is only one way of life! The Greek word translated **ways** is found one hundred and one times in the New Testament. However, nearly one-third of all occurrences are found in Luke's writings. Since the statement in our passage is coming from the lips of Christ (a Messianic Psalm), it might help us to consider two other major occurrences where He used this imagery.

In the Sermon on the Mount Jesus declared, *"Enter by the narrow gate; for wide is the gate and broad is the way that leads to destruction, and there are many who go in by it. Because narrow is the gate and difficult is the way which leads to life, and there are few who find it"* (Matthew 7:13-14). The danger of these two verses is to interpret them out of their context. One could conclude that there are two possibilities with two destinations. It is my responsibility to "find" the path which leads to life. It is like trying to find a path in difficult terrain, or coming across a narrow entry after a lengthy search. This would reduce the Scriptures to a road map which I must follow explicitly without detours.

However, we must view these two verses (Matthew 7:13-14) in light of their context, the Sermon on the Mount. Jesus establishes the "seeking-finding" concept. Even at the end of these two verses, He says, *"and there are few who find it,"* (Matthew 7:14). In the verses just prior to this statement (Matthew 7:7-12), Jesus focuses on the "seeking-finding" concept. He indicates that "finding" is guaranteed in the "seeking." "Opening" is certain in the "knocking!" "Receiving" is to be expected in the "asking!" He stated this same concept earlier (Matthew 6:33). The focus of the Sermon on the Mount is not the road map, performance list, or self-searching routine. It is the mystery of the Divine action whereby if we seek (respond) He will find us!

There are those Bible scholars who believe the great theme or proposition of the Sermon on the Mount is the opening Beatitude: *Blessed are the poor in spirit, For theirs is the Kingdom of heaven (Matthew 5:3).*

Those who have nothing with which to buy, no status by which to claim, and no merit by which to demand have the Kingdom of God as their own!

Narrow is the gate and difficult is the way is because it runs cross grain to our very self-sourcing nature. Pride demands that we must find; brokenness requires we must be found. Self-accomplishment requires the claim of achievement; seeking (responding) implies accepting. Self-reliance promotes the "I must do it" attitude; inability demands "I must be enabled." This is "relational" language. The imagery of the *way* is not about the discovery of a road and carefully walking in this safe path. It is about Christ who is *the way, the truth, and the life* (John 14:6).

This brings us to another strong declaration of Jesus concerning the *way* (John 14:6). Your understanding of the context is essential in light of its statement. In John's account of the Gospel these chapters (14, 15 and 16) are a long discourse given by Jesus in the upper room. He is at the moment of betrayal and crucifixion. The focus of the discourse is the purpose for all that will take place in the next few days. His death, resurrection and ascension will be to accomplish the fullness of the Spirit.

Jesus said, *"I will pray the Father, and He will give you another Helper, that He may abide with you forever – the Spirit of truth, whom the world cannot receive, because it neither sees Him nor knows Him; but you know Him, for He dwells with you and will be in you. I will not leave you orphans; I will come to you,"* (John 14:16-18). This statement is not about His second coming. It is about the outside God getting inside. This is Pentecost.

Jesus begins His discourse by encouraging His disciples. He understands their dismay over His immanent departure, but it is only because they do not fully comprehend all He has tried to teach them (John 14:1). In the Father's household (family) there are many dwelling places, not mansions (John 14:2). Up to this time, the disciples have only seen one dwelling place; that is Jesus. He is filled with the Spirit. Jesus is going to go away (crucifixion, resurrection and ascension) in order to prepare more dwelling places. He is going to prepare them to become dwelling places. If Jesus participates in the difficulty of going away and prepares them as dwelling places, He will come again (not second coming) and receive (a Greek word always used regarding people, a term of intimacy) them to Himself (John 14:3). The result will be that where He is (state of being) they will also be (state of being). Where He goes, they know. They also know the *way* (John 14:4).

Thomas totally misses the point (John 14:5). Road maps, destinations, and traveling dominate His thoughts. From this view He does not know where Jesus is going or how he could get here. Jesus explains, *"I am the way, the truth, and the life. No one comes to the Father except through Me"* (John 14:6). In the rest of the three chapters

(John 14, 15 and 16) Jesus speaks of the indwelling of the Spirit of Christ. What Jesus accomplished for us is found in who He is. The *way* is not about road maps and traveling, but about intimacy and relationship.

One hundred and twenty disciples have received the fullness of the Holy Spirit. A large crowd of Jews witness this outpouring. Peter is moved upon by the Holy Spirit to give an explanation. His entire sermon focuses on Jesus as the clarification. *Jesus of Nazareth, a Man* is filled with the Father who sources His life, His death, and His resurrection (Acts2:22-24). It was the absolute CONCENTRATION (Acts 2:25) of the Father that enabled this spiritual condition in the Son. The result of this was CELEBRATION (Acts 2:26), which was high-spirited fun permeating Jesus' entire being. As Jesus breaks into worship, He addresses the Father. His worship reveals the depth of His COMMUNION (Acts 2:27) with the Father. They are so welded together, they cannot be separated. In the depth of their relationship there is found a paralleled depth of COMMUNICATION (Acts 2:28). As the Father and Son embrace they explicitly reveal life. It is life in abundance, in the eternal, and in every aspect of Jesus' being. It is *the way of life*. He did not find this in performance or the mapping of travel. He found it in the intimacy of the embrace and the Father in His eye. This is present in Jesus. It was given to the disciples. It is promised to you!

15

THE ULTIMATE GOAL

ACTS 2:28

In my younger days of ministry, I was somewhat repelled by those who had a futuristic view of Christianity. During revivals in those days, the closing night would always be focused on heaven. The song evangelist would feature our future in glory land and the old saints would get blessed. None of this seemed to resonate with me. I thought probably it was just my age and this would change as I got older. Now I am "old" but find my feelings the same.

It is very dangerous to speak like this due to misunderstanding. Not everyone is in the same place. We are certainly not against the blessings and plans of God for the future in eternity. However, the focus for the future has often been streets of gold in front of great mansions. This is not unlike many of the world religions which have proposed the future life will abundantly provide those things we sacrificed or do not have in the present. Often our expectations of the future have been an expansion of the present focus. Could the focus on life without pain, suffering, and death in the future be a product of the circumstances we are struggling with in the present? Could the physical comfort of big mansions in the future life be a result of the focus on a materialistic struggle in the present? While this may not be evil, it should not be the determining factor of our perspective.

There is a Biblical principle which remains true in all of the writers of the New Testament. Eternal life is not that which is to come, but is that which is started now. John highlights this repeatedly in his Gospel account. Our life in eternity is an expansion of this life. We must not view them as separate or different lives. Eighty years on this earth is really brief compared to the infinite eternal life. Yet, it is very significant. It is so valuable we must embrace it as much as we look forward to eternal life. This life is not one thing and eternal life another. They are stages to the same living experience. One is the expansion of the same substance experienced in the other.

We do not consider our childhood as one life and our adulthood as a separate or different life. Our childhood is very brief in comparison to the time span of adulthood. However, it is in this childhood that the very roots of adulthood are found. Our responses, concepts, and attitudes of life are all shaped in our childhood. The patterns we establish in this period become a determining factor in the quality of our adult living. While childhood may be vague in our memory, it is very influential and is not considered a separate life. So it is with the linkage between our life in this time zone and our eternal life. One does not live one way in this time zone and then have a different life in eternity. The patterns, direction, and style of life are determined in our present life and will be expanded in eternity. Eternity is an expansion of what we are already experiencing in this life!

This is the concept expressed by the Messiah in our passage. Peter explains to the Jews of the Dispersion the essence of Pentecost. *Jesus of Nazareth, a Man* is his explanation. Jesus is sourced by the Father in the same exact manner we are to be sourced by Jesus. Everything expressed in Jesus is promised to us. However, we must have the same spiritual condition which allows this sourcing. It is the same spiritual condition found in Jesus. This is described for us by Jesus in a Messianic Psalm (Psalm 16:8-11) which is quoted by Peter (Acts 2:25-28).

Jesus was totally focused on the Father (CONCENTRATION, Acts 2:25). The Father was the pivotal point of influence and resource. Jesus was captured, mastered, and obsessed by the Father. During this focus there was a CELEBRATION taking place (Acts 2:26). It was high-spirited fun as they made merry. This happened within Jesus and the Father. It spread from His heart, to His emotion, to His countenance, and to the very tone of His life. Even His physical body found resource in this merriment. The strength of this condition spilled forth into worship. It was an expression of the depth of the COMMUNION between them (Acts 2:27). The Father and Son are inseparable. The depth of this relationship is expressed in COMMUNICATION (Acts 2:28). The Father was in Jesus' eye (Acts 2:25), then in His heart (Acts 2:26). The Father was in His cell structure (Acts 2:27) and even in His ear (Acts 2:28).

Communication is not accomplished until the recipient has understood. The communication is determined by the depth of the intimacy between them. Jesus spoke of this to His disciples in the upper room before His crucifixion. He said, *"However, when He, the Spirit of truth, has come, He will guide you into all truth;"* (John 16:13). It is a causative statement. The Holy Spirit is going to wrap His arm around you and cause you to be brought into the full knowledge and understanding of the Person of Jesus. In the depth of the union with our heart, He knows how to reveal Himself to us! Obviously the *way of life* is Jesus. So the opening statement in our passage gives expression to this revelation. *You have made known to me the ways of life;* (Acts 2:28).

There is one more clear statement in our passage. It is the climax of His expression of the intimacy between the Father and the Son. He cries, *"You will make me full of joy in Your presence"* (Acts 2:28). In many ways this statement becomes the great summary of everything Jesus has already spoken in the Messianic Psalm. He is expressing one more time the details of His spiritual condition.

The Greek verb of this great statement is translated, *You will make full.* Notice it is in the future tense. In the Greek language the future tense has a very significant aspect about it. The future tense is the only tense which expresses only a level of time. It does not refer to the completion or duration of an action. If this statement (Acts 2:28) is really a summary of the entire Psalm, the verb tense used in the various explanations up to this point are all going to take place in the future as well. The past tense refers to what has taken place in my history and has end. The present tense gives a picture of now which also is quickly completed. The future announces the continuation in the days ahead with no prospect of ending.

In this last statement, Jesus grasps all He has experienced with the Father and proclaims it will continue in the future. Whatever happens in the resurrection, ascension, and exaltation will be a continuation of what He has already been experiencing. He may have new circumstances with new surroundings, but what has been His life up to this point will continue to be His life in the future. What sources Him in these days of earthly ministry will continue to source Him in the eternal dwelling.

In the future, the Father *will make full*. The Greek word comes from the idea "to complete" or "to finish." It means to fill, supply abundantly with something, impart richly, or to permeate and invade. This same Greek word is used in connection with the devil. He has the ability to activate this in our lives. But Peter said, *"Ananias, why has Satan filled your heart to lie to the Holy Spirit and keep back part of the price of the land for yourself?"* (Acts 5:3). Satan desires to fill, permeate, and complete his work in us. Will this not also be true of eternity? If Satan is allowed to accomplish this in my present life, why would he not continue it in the future? Eternity is an expansion of what I now experience!

This same Greek word is used by Luke as a description of the Pentecost event. *And suddenly there came a sound from heaven, as of a rushing mighty wind, and it filled the whole house where they were sitting* (Acts 2:2). He uses the imagery of an echo (Greek word for *sound*). The fullness of the Holy Spirit has come from the Father and is rebounding and reflecting from the believer. The believer is *filled*. You will remember from previous studies this word is contrasted with the Greek word translated "filled" in verse four. This Greek word is used in verse two as well as in our study verse and it paints the picture of a container being filled with content. The outside content is coming inside the container. It is *filled*!

It cannot be an accident that Jesus uses this same word to describe what will take place in His future life. Peter's explanation of Pentecost is about Jesus. What happened in the life of Jesus is now happening in one hundred and twenty disciples. It is now promised to us. Jesus is sourced by the Father. This sourcing is now ours to claim. Evidently it is not just a time zone sourcing. The Father did not give this to *Jesus of Nazareth, a Man* because He needed it to make it through this life. When Jesus ascended to the right hand of the Father as *a Man*, did He no longer need this sourcing of God's life? No, He needs this same sourcing in the heavenly realms. The fullness of the Spirit defines human beings! We will not cease to be human beings in the eternal realms; we will not become angels. We will be people filled and sourced by God. Jesus is the prototype.

Peter continues in his sermon to highlight the sourcing of the Father through Jesus even after death. Jesus did not raise Himself from the dead, but was raised by the Father (Acts 2:24; 2:32). In eternity Jesus is to occupy a position at the right hand of the Father. In this position He is going to be sourced by the Father. Peter preached, *"Therefore being exalted to the right hand of God, and having received from the Father the promise of the Holy Spirit, He poured out this which you now see and hear,"* (Acts 2:33). The redemptive work to mankind continues in Pentecost, being sourced by the Father through Jesus. The Father is the source of the outpouring of the Holy Spirit!

This is promised to us in eternity as well. As we

experience the fullness of the Holy Spirit here, we will experience it there. The spiritual experience we have now will be our spiritual experience in eternity. It is an expansion of His Divine presence. If you and I do not have the sourcing of the Spirit in this present life, we will not experience it in the life to come! Death is not a cure. It is certainly not a magic wand which miraculously transforms me. It is a transition from this stage of my life to another.

As Jesus highlights this continuation into the future, He focuses on two important issues which simply verify this truth. First, there is *"You will make me full of joy,"* (Acts 2:28). This is very significant. The Greek word translated *joy* is the same Greek word translated *rejoiced* (Acts 2:26). Jesus describes His spiritual condition which allows the Father to source Him in His earthly ministry. The Father is in His eye (CONCENTRATION – Acts 2:25). The more Jesus sees the Father the more Jesus loves the Father. The Father draws Jesus into His very presence. The intimacy and oneness is on the highest level. He is one with the Father. The oneness has a natural result. It is CELEBRATION. *"Therefore my heart rejoiced, and my tongue was glad;"* (Acts 2:26). The Greek word translated *rejoiced* comes from a root word meaning "well minded." It is not the same "rejoice" to which Paul refers in his writings. It is often translated "merry." In the English dictionary it means "high-spirited fun." Jesus describes His life on this earth as one of intimacy with the Father that results in high-spirited fun at the heart of His being.

Now He restates this same thought (Acts 2:28). In the future, the same spiritual condition will exist. He will no longer be in this time zone, but He will continue to be sourced by the Father. Eternity for Him will be an expansion of what He is already experiencing in this present world. Intimacy with the Father will continue to result in a "well mind" and a heart that is filled with "high-spirited fun." The same relationship Jesus has had with the Father will continue into eternity. As the Father has sourced Jesus in earthly living, so He will source Him in eternal living!

This is promised to you and to me. Peter explains the Pentecost event. What is taking place in the lives of one hundred and twenty believers is what Jesus experienced. This is the Promise of the Father, and it is now ours. It is ours forever. Our bodies cannot tolerate the stress or the anxiety of sourcing our own lives. Our minds collapse under the pressure of responsibility when we are alone. We were designed for the indwelling of the Father. Jesus is the pattern. His life was not the removal of conflict, battle, or strife. It was His dependency on the sourcing of the Father in the midst of all circumstances. In the middle of upheaval, there is high-spirited fun at the core of His living. If this is not true now, it will not be accomplished in death. Death is a transition of what we are now into we will be forever. Eternity is a continuation of our present spiritual patterns and directions.

There is a second thought which verifies this same truth. Jesus is saying, *"You will make me full of joy in Your presence,"* (Acts 2:28). His choice of words is very significant. He has restated the CELEBRATION of merriment which has come as a result of the intimacy He has with His Father. Now He is going to restate His CONCENTRATION on the Father. The same Greek word translated *presence* in our verse (Acts 2:28) is used by Jesus in His beginning statement. He said, *"I foresaw the Lord always before my face,"* (Acts 2:25). ***Presence*** and ***before face*** are translated from the same Greek word.

This Messianic Psalm was originally written in Hebrew and then translated into Greek. In the Hebrew language there was no word for ***presence***. They used the idea of "being in your face." As it was translated into the Greek language, a compound word was used. The first word indicates motion toward and the second word means the area around the eye. It expresses the idea of coming into or toward your eye (face). Jesus is expressing His CONCENTRATION on the Father at the beginning of this Messianic Psalm. The Father has gotten in His eye. He could not see anything else. Everything else is overshadowed by the Father's presence. The Father is the center point of everything that happens in His life. The entire life of Jesus revolves around the Father. He simply cannot see anything else.

This concept is highlighted with the use of the Greek word translated "in" as found in our passage (Acts 2:28). It is an unfortunate translation because it confuses us with the first statement of Christ (Acts 2:26). As Jesus spoke of His CONCENTRATION on the Father He used the Greek word which is translated "in." In our translation it is stated as ***before***. This gives us the picture of remaining or no movement. The Father has come to the very eye of Christ and is dwelling there! Now in this concluding statement Jesus uses the Greek word which is normally translated "with" (Acts 2:28). It is a word which expresses a form of relationship. The relationship is usually personal. It designates the person in whose fellowship or accompaniment something takes place.

Jesus, in his final hours before the crucifixion, opens His heart to the disciples. In relating the fullness of the Spirit who will come to be with them, He says, *"And I will pray the Father, and He will give you another Helper, that He may abide with you forever"* (John 14:16). He is not speaking of the Holy Spirit simply accompanying the believer. It is not in the sense of a guardian angel that protects us from unseen dangers. He will be "with" us in the sense of relationship. Listen to the final statement of the Apostle Paul in his second letter to the Corinthians. He wrote, *The grace of the Lord Jesus Christ, and the love of God, and the communion of the Holy Spirit be with you all. Amen.* (2 Corinthians 13:14). This is not a desire that our experience with God would be as one carrying a rabbit's foot or four leaf clover. This is relational. To experience the Trinity in intimacy is the heart of Christianity. It is then that grace is known, love is experienced, and oneness of communication is embraced.

The Messiah is expressing His present experience of this depth of relationship in His opening statement (Acts 2:25). The Father is in His eye. The Father remains the single focus of Jesus' life. This is the spiritual condition which allows the sourcing of the Spirit. Now as He closes this great statement He boldly proclaims this will continue in the future. As He ascends to the right hand of the Father and assumes His rightful place as King of the Kingdom, this will continue. This intimacy between them is not only a time zone embrace, but an eternal oneness. What has been experienced in the present will follow into eternity.

Peter explains Pentecost to us. Jesus is the explanation. As the Father sourced Jesus, He will also source us. We must have the same spiritual condition Jesus had. As this is established in the present time zone and flows into the eternal realms for Jesus, so what is established in our present will expand in our eternity. What is your intimacy level with Jesus now? Will you be satisfied with this level when He comes again?

Made in United States
Troutdale, OR
11/11/2024

24662478R00096